The
SOUP SISTERS
Cookbook

Beet, Apple and Potato Soup (page 150)

The
SOUP SISTERS
Cookbook

100 SIMPLE RECIPES TO WARM HEARTS . . .
ONE BOWL AT A TIME

EDITED BY

SHARON HAPTON

with PIERRE A. LAMIELLE

appetite
by RANDOM HOUSE

Library and Archives of Canada Cataloguing in Publication is available upon request

ISBN: 978-0-449-01559-9

Squash, Pear and Parsnip with Ginger recipe (page 36) Copyright © 1997 dee Hobsbawn-Smith

Cover and text design: Leah Springate
Cover image (and photo on page 166): Shallon Cunningham, Salt Photography
Food photography and styling: Julie Van Rosendaal

Printed and bound in China

Published in Canada by Appetite by Random House,
a division of Random House of Canada Limited

www.randomhouse.ca

10 9 8

Contents

The Power of Soup

I am a soup maker. For most of my adult life, I have taken care of family and friends with soup. If someone was down or needed some extra care, I would show up at their door, most often unannounced, with soup. I knew that this simple gesture had the power to change their day, and in the process of making the soup, I was letting them know how much I cared. The whole exchange—the soup making, the visit, the comfort it provided and appreciation it returned—created a fulfilling cycle of giving.

Coming to this realization of my identity as "soup maker" was a process in and of itself. It all started back when I was facing the prospect of an empty nest. The time was fast approaching and was going to coincide with a milestone birthday (my 50th). I had spent a lot of time thinking about what it was going to feel like and how exactly my life would change. I didn't have any huge obstacles to overcome other than the ones I was beginning to create in my own mind. I thought that I needed to reinvent myself and create some greater meaning in who I was and what I did. My husband and I had a wonderful family business that we had grown together, but after 30 successful years, it didn't require all that much of me anymore. I spent the next two years writing down various ideas, so that when the time came for my kids to leave for university, I wouldn't suddenly be faced with what I referred to as "my giant nurture void."

One day, as I realized that I wasn't ever really going to be a ballerina (or follow any other childhood fantasy career that I may have secretly longed for), I had a giant epiphany. I was looking everywhere but the obvious place. I realized that the one thing I had quite literally been doing for as long as I could remember was making soup for the people I cared about. When a close artist friend's house burned to the ground, I showed up every week at her temporary home with different beautiful colors of soup. When another girlfriend's husband was suffering through chemotherapy, I took them nourishing soup. When another friend was beyond stressed by a personal crisis, I brought soup so she could serve it to her family and know that she was still taking care of them. It was a quiet gesture that delivered a resounding message of love and concern.

I had seen the results over and over of the power of soup and the profound comfort contained in every delivery. So I asked myself, "Why couldn't this be bigger? Why couldn't people everywhere be making soup to nurture and nourish others?" That day, when the inspiration hit during one of my regular solo walks, I came home and asked my then 18-year-old daughter what she thought of the name *Soup Sisters*. She let me know in no uncertain terms that it was incredibly corny! I had an action plan simmering for my 50th birthday.

The beauty of getting older is that we finally begin to overcome our fear about the success or failure of an idea. Finally, we can shed our worries about how something looks or doesn't look to others and feel emboldened to be our authentic selves. So, on my 50th, I invited 30 girlfriends to a soup-making birthday party held at a professional culinary facility and invited the executive director of our local women's shelter to speak, as we were going to donate soup (lots of it) to the women and children in the shelter. That evening with my wonderful friends was the prototype for Soup Sisters.

I had seen the results over and over of the power of soup and the profound comfort contained in every delivery.

Something completely magical took place in the room that night. From that moment, we were all given a greater purpose to make the best soup that we could for people whom we didn't know, whose lives had been affected by domestic abuse and family violence. Our soup would be delivered to women who may have been the ones providing nurturing meals for their family. We were together making soup as a way of reaching out to them. We would prepare that nourishing meal for their family because they weren't able to make it themselves.

I'll never forget when the time came to ladle hundreds of bowls of soup that would be delivered to the shelter the next day. I was absolutely awestruck by what we had accomplished, and all while we were having the greatest time together. The snapshot in my mind of that moment, which I have now looked at hundreds of times, always has the same effect on me. It's our way of making a gesture of care and concern at the grassroots level for the many women and children who suffer abuse. We are letting them know that we are taking a stand against family violence and domestic abuse while offering them the comfort and healing warmth that comes from wholesome soup. There is a heartfelt message with that bowl of soup that says, "We care. You aren't alone and you have the support of a community on your journey toward a life free from abuse."

Here was the recipe for Soup Sisters. All it took was for me to realize that I didn't need to look beyond my truest self, that what I was looking for had always been inside me just waiting to be recognized. After all, I am, and always have been, a soup maker.

Yours in soup,

Sharon Hapton
Founder, Soup Sisters and Broth Brothers

Welcome

Welcome to *The Soup Sisters Cookbook*, a collective melting pot that combines favorite recipes from many of our Soup Sisters and Broth Brothers volunteers with recipes from more than 50 chefs and food professionals. This book is chock-full of fantastic recipes, stirred together to create a heartwarming collection that was made possible only through the kindness of our contributors. In here, you'll find soups for fall, winter, spring and summer, so that, whatever the season, you know there's a soup to suit.

To fit all the recipes into this one big book we've streamlined them so that most fit on one page. Instead of explaining 20 times how to dice an onion or purée a soup, we've put all those tips and techniques up front for you to cross-reference. If you need help figuring out how to cut up a cauliflower or brown some meat, the Soup-Making Techniques section will show you how.

Most of the recipes will make between four and eight servings, but of course this also depends on the size of your appetite! Soup leftovers are perfect for freezing and we've included instructions for how to do that. Alternatively, you can enjoy one bowl yourself and give the rest away to someone you care about. As the Soup Sisters say: Soup it forward!

Throughout the book you'll discover the following icons, designed to help you get to the heart of the recipe with just a quick glance:

 Vegetarian means that nothing in the soup ever said anything like "oink," "cluck" or "moo." Some of our vegetarian soups might include eggs and/or dairy products, so be sure to read the recipe carefully if these are foods you'd rather live without.

 Vegan means that all of the ingredients in the soup are derived from vegetables or grains, and will be completely free of all dairy products and eggs.

 Gluten-free means no sneaky wheat snuck into this soup. Sometimes it tiptoes into soup in the form of flour, whole grains or bread, but not for the recipes with this icon attached.

You'll also notice these lovely little icons peppered among the recipes:

A wooden spoon indicates a helpful hint or tip that gives you a little more detail about the recipe, for example, a serving suggestion or information on alternative ingredients.

A chef's hat highlights a story, tip or tale that comes direct from the chef, food professional or Soup Sister who contributed the recipe. This could be something about the history of the soup, or a memory about cooking it.

Getting Started

If your pantry, vegetable basket and fridge are fully stocked, it's easy to make soup at a moment's notice. Here are our tips for what you'll need.

THE PANTRY

Having a well-stocked pantry is like packing a proper first aid kit. With these essentials, you'll have everything you need waiting for you right there in your kitchen, anytime you want to stir up some soup.

Dried herbs and spices

- allspice, ground
- basil, dried
- bay leaves
- cardamom, whole and ground
- cayenne pepper
- chili powder
- cinnamon, ground
- cinnamon sticks
- cloves (whole)
- coriander, ground
- coriander seeds (whole)
- cumin, ground
- cumin seeds (whole)
- curry powder
- nutmeg (ground nutmeg, or whole nutmeg that you freshly grate yourself)
- oregano, dried
- paprika, Hungarian sweet
- paprika, Spanish sweet smoked
- peppercorns, black (whole)
- peppercorns, white (whole)
- red chili flakes
- thyme, dried
- turmeric

Beans and lentils

Canned beans make it much simpler to whip up a batch of soup fast without having to go through the soaking or rehydrating process that dried beans need. We do, however, like to keep a variety of dried beans around, too. (For more on soaking and precooking beans see page 19.)

Dried lentils and split peas don't need to be soaked before using, and they cook more quickly than beans. They add heartiness to any soup and are great to have on hand.

Rice and pasta

Having an assortment of different types of rice is great for soup making: arborio can thicken a bisque; brown rice can beef up a chili. And having pasta in a variety of shapes and sizes is sure to add diversity to your soup servings: use up the last few handfuls of macaroni in a pot of minestrone, or add alphabet-shaped pasta when you want to send secret messages in your soup.

Stock

We have included a full section on making stocks from scratch, guaranteed to add extra deliciousness to your soups. If you don't have time to make these, keep some store-bought stock in your cupboard instead—we prefer the organic varieties. You can use stock cubes, too, when you're really in a pinch. Just remember that ready-made stock and stock cubes usually contain higher amounts of sodium, which means you won't have to add as much salt when you're souping.

Oils

Grapeseed and canola oil are great for frying at high temperatures. Use regular olive oil if you're cooking over lower temps, and keep that good fruity extra virgin olive oil for drizzling on top of a soup, or dipping your bread in.

Crackers

There are few things finer than a cracker for crumbling into or eating with your soup.

Salt

Any salt will do for seasoning soup, no matter what a salt seller may tell you. Expensive salts come in cool colors, some have neat textures and others have flavors like smoke or truffle. These can be saved and used to garnish a soup as a final flourish. Stick with good old kosher or sea salt (or even table salt, in a pinch) to make everything taste delicious when cooking.

(Also, be sure to read up on how to "salt to taste" on page 12.)

Pepper

Freshly ground black pepper is the pepper to use when souping. Mixtures of differently colored peppercorns can be good, too. Try to use white pepper only in creamy pale-colored soups that need to be kept quite pristine.

THE VEGETABLE BASKET

Be sure to always have carrots, celery and onions on hand. They all keep for a long time and if they start to look a little bit limp, that's when they're perfect for tossing into a batch of stock.

Squash (especially butternut) and root vegetables, like potatoes and rutabaga, will keep most of the winter in a cool dry cupboard, so they're good to keep around and especially handy to have if you get snowed in.

Garlic is a must-have too. If you end up with little green sprouts poking out of the top of the bulb, don't worry, you can pop those in the stockpot, too.

THE FRIDGE/FREEZER

Not every soup ingredient will be waiting for you in the pantry. Fresh, bright flavor often comes from fresh, bright ingredients that have to be stored in the fridge or freezer.

Herbs

Fresh herbs are irreplaceable. The beautiful bright green bouquet of fresh herbs can never be matched by dried herbs.

Fresh parsley, cilantro and basil are perfect for finely chopping and stirring into your soups at the last minute. Keep fresh herbs in your vegetable crisper or, if you have a green thumb, grow them on your windowsill.

Lemons

Lemons are bright and fresh and come with two awesome ingredients in one nifty yellow package. You can use a zester to remove the powerfully aromatic zest from the outside of a lemon, and then juice the fruit to harvest the tart lemon juice inside to add a lovely balance and brightness to your soups.

Butter

Only butter is butter. It's just one of those ingredients that cannot be substituted. Margarine is not butter; I repeat, only butter is butter. You can really taste the difference!

Bacon

There are few ingredients that can elevate soup to the next level as quickly as bacon. Whether you fry it in with your mirepoix (see page 22), cook with the bacon's rendered fat or top your soup with crunchy bacon bits, it's only going to make your soup (and your life) taste better.

Cream

It's rare that milk is called for in soup. That's because cream makes more sense. It quickly smooths out flavors, gives silky unctuous texture and makes your soup feel like a special occasion.

Frozen stock

Look at all that lovely homemade stock you made after reading pages 23 to 25! Now you can make soup anytime you like and feel all warm and fuzzy knowing that it's the most homemade soup you can possibly make. For tips on how to freeze soup and stock, turn to page 21.

ESSENTIAL EQUIPMENT

Pots
Heavy-bottomed stainless steel pots make the soup world go round. The thicker the bottom of the pot, the better it will conduct heat and the more control you'll have over browning veg and boiling soup. It helps to have a variety of sizes of pots for making big batches of stock or reheating small portions of soup for dinner.

Knives
Dull knives are dangerous because they slip around and you don't know where they're going to go. A sharp knife goes where you tell it to and ensures you get nice, even cuts, so you will get nice, even cooking and nice, even soup. Invest in good knives and learn how to sharpen them.

Cutting boards
Softwood or plastic cutting boards are best because that glass, marble or hard composite board is dulling your knife every time you cut a carrot.

Vegetable peelers

There are lots of shapes and sizes of peelers. The fastest and most efficient is the Y-shaped or speed peeler. Get one with a good grip and it will peel things very effectively.

Sieve

A large fine-mesh sieve is great for straining impurities out of stock and for ensuring puréed soups are as smooth as can be.

Cheesecloth

Cheesecloth is handy for tying up little bouquet garni bundles (see page 22). It's also useful for lining a sieve when you want to strain the teensiest impurities out of your stock.

Spoons, ladles and whisks

Big sturdy wooden spoons are good for lots of heavy stirring and even better for swatting people if they try to steal any crunchy bacon bits. Slotted metal spoons are great for taking out solid things and leaving the liquid behind. Ladles should hold a full serving of soup, be made of metal and hopefully have a little hook at the end to hang them from. And whisks are sometimes needed for soup; they should be sturdy and hefty and metal.

Little bowls

Mise en place is the term chefs use to describe what they do before they start cooking: put everything in its place. And, the "place" they're talking about is little bowls. Do you have diced carrots that need to be put in their place? Stick 'em in a little bowl. Where does chopped cilantro go? In a little bowl. Little bowls are super-handy for getting all your ingredients prepped and ready to go.

Little plates

Putting a little plate beside your stove while you cook is a great idea. You can rest your dirty spoons and soupy ladles on it (if you don't have a spoon rest) or put a bouquet garni (see page 22) on it, and it keeps things super-clean and tidy.

Tasting spoons

It's a great idea to have a small container near the stove full of tasting spoons. Handy little spoons are great for when you are adjusting the taste of your soup. You should use a clean spoon for each taste and make sure you don't put the dirty spoons back in with the clean ones!

Countertop blender vs. immersion blender

When it comes to puréeing soup, here are your two best choices:

A countertop blender is the kind with a goblet that sits on a motorized base. It will give you the smoothest soup, but there are some safety concerns to consider (check these out on page 20). In any event, make sure your blender has progressive speeds so you can slowly turn up the dial to get the smoothest of purées.

An immersion blender (sometimes called a hand blender or wand blender) is the kind you submerge in a pot of soup, switch on and move around in the pot to purée the soup. An immersion blender is useful, but it takes longer to purée a soup this way, and the soup may not be perfectly smooth as with a countertop blender. On the plus side, immersion blenders are easy to clean and fun to swirl around.

Read up on soup puréeing tips on page 20.

SOUP-MAKING TECHNIQUES

Throughout this book you'll find that we've kept the instructions in the recipes very short and concise. And they will be peppered with quick requests to "purée until smooth" or "add 1 clove garlic, crushed." In this section, we walk you through these steps and provide more in-depth information, so you have what you need to make those things happen.

Salt to taste

Salting to taste can be a bit of a learning experience and it always varies based on your personal palate. When salting a soup, remember that you can add salt but you can't take it back out. If you oversalt there is little you can do to fix it.

Add salt at the very end of soup making because if you salt the soup perfectly halfway through cooking and the stock reduces, you'll end up with a salty soup. Plumes of steam will have floated away while the heavy salt stayed in the pot.

Add salt a bit at a time, stir the soup around and then taste it. When your tongue says "Wow, delicious!" you'll know you've added the right amount of salt.

Pepper to taste

Adding pepper to taste is similar to adding salt, although the effect of pepper takes a little longer to permeate the soup. If you add pepper, wait a couple of minutes before you taste it.

Better still, just put the pepper grinder on the table and let folks have their way with it.

1 onion, diced

1. Slice the top off your onion.
2. Just barely shave the root end off, ensuring the whole thing stays together for the cutting process.
3. Cut your onion in half, straight through the middle of the root end to the top.
4. Peel the onion halves.
5. Lay the onion halves on their flat sides.
6. Make lengthwise radial cuts, cutting only two-thirds of the way to the root end.
7. Slice the onion again crosswise (90 degrees to your original cuts), and marvel at your perfect dice.
8. Repeat with the remaining onion half.

Want smaller dice? Make your cuts closer together.
Want bigger dice? Make your cuts farther apart.

1 leek, white and pale green parts only, washed and sliced

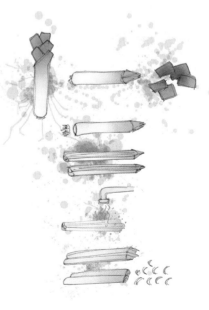

1. Trim off the dark green ends of the leek.
2. Barely shave the roots off the root end.
3. Split the leek down the middle lengthwise.
4. Clean the leek under cold running water, pulling back the leaves to get rid of any trapped dirt.
5. Shake off any excess water.
6. Slice the leek thinly crosswise, discarding the root end.

1 carrot, diced

1. Hold the carrot perpendicular to the cutting board and run the peeler down the carrot to peel it.
2. Cut the carrot into 3-inch (8 cm) pieces.
3. Cut off four sides of each piece to square them up.
4. Cut each squared piece of carrot lengthwise into ½-inch (1 cm) slices.
5. Cut the slices crosswise to make batons.
6. Cut the batons into dice.

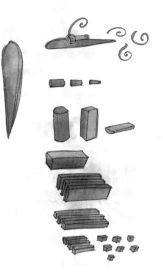

1 stalk celery, diced

1. Trim the celery stalk crosswise into 3-inch (8 cm) pieces.
2. Slice each piece lengthwise into batons.
3. Cut the batons into dice.

1 sweet red (or green) pepper, diced

1. Cut the pepper in half.
2. Remove the stem and seeds.
3. Slice the pepper into strips.
4. Cut the slices into dice.

1 tomato, peeled, seeded and diced

To peel:

1. Put a big pot of water on to boil and have ready a bowlful of icy water.
2. Cut a small X in the bottom of the tomato.
3. When the water boils, drop the tomato in the pot.
4. After 30 seconds, scoop out the tomato and dunk it immediately into the ice water.
5. Remove the tomato from the ice water, then peel off the skin.

To seed:

1. Cut the tomatoes into quarters.
2. Use a small pairing knife to cut out the seeds.

To dice:

1. Cut the tomato quarters into long strips.
2. Cut the strips crosswise into dice.

1 chili, finely diced

Sometimes putting a whole chili pepper into a soup while it cooks adds enough heat. Just remember to take it out before you serve the soup or you'll be dishing up a firecracker to someone. **Warning:** Whatever you do, don't go handling a hot pepper then scratch your eye or any other part of your face. The burn can be excruciating. Immediately after handling a hot pepper, wash your hands really well with lots of warm, soapy water, then wash them again.

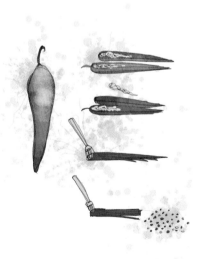

1. Split the chili lengthwise.
2. To avoid a major heat rush, slice out the white membranes and seeds.
3. Use a fork to hold one end of the pepper in place on your cutting board, then cut it into long strips, holding the strips together at one end with the fork.
4. Cut the long strips crosswise into small dice.

1 clove garlic, crushed/sliced/finely chopped/minced

To crush:
- Place the flat side of your knife on the unpeeled clove of garlic and press down with your palm to crush it. Peel off and discard the skin.

To slice:
- Use a sharp knife to slice a peeled clove of garlic into thin strips.

To finely chop:
- Use a sharp knife and, holding the tip of the knife against the cutting board, move the knife up and down and from side to side to chop a peeled clove of garlic into tiny pieces.

To mince:
- For a finer texture that lets the garlic just melt into any soup, use a Microplane grater to grate a peeled clove of garlic into a fine pulp. Or finely chop the garlic then use the flat side of your knife to crush the chopped garlic into a fine pulp.

Fresh ginger, grated

1. Use the inside edge of the tip of a spoon to peel a piece of fresh ginger.
2. With a zester or Microplane grater, grate the ginger into a fine pulp.

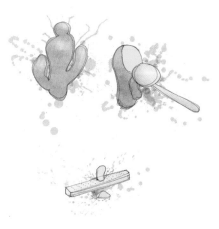

Prepping cauliflower/broccoli

1. Trim away any leaves with a small paring knife.
2. Use the paring knife to split the stem down the middle; don't cut the florets, just split the stem from the underside.
3. Pry open each half of the stem to split the cauliflower/broccoli evenly down the middle.
4. Continue splitting the stems in half and pulling them apart until you get to the size of florets you're looking for.

Butternut squash, diced

1. Use a heavy-duty knife to cut the ends off the butternut squash.
2. Cut the squash into two pieces where the round part of the squash joins the long part.
3. Cut the round section in half, and with a spoon, scoop out the seeds and gunk.
4. Use your knife to remove the peel from all three pieces of squash.
5. Now you have big pieces that can be cut into smaller dice.

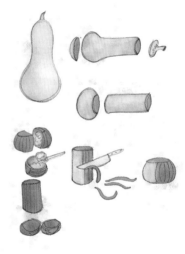

Herbs, roughly/finely chopped

1. If the herb has a tough woody stem, remove all the leaves from the stem. Pile the leaves together.
2. Make several chops in one direction and you're done. Don't get crazy with too much chopping.
3. If the herb has a nice soft stem, like cilantro or parsley, it's a lot easier: hold your bunch by the stem ends and chop through once. Discard the stems.
4. For finely chopped, continue chopping the herbs until you get a nice finely chopped pile.

Zest of 1 lime/orange/lemon

1. Use a zester, rasp or Microplane grater to shave off a nice fine sprinkling of the colorful skin of your citrus.
2. Once you get down to the white bit, you can stop. That white stuff is called the pith, and it's bitter and not lovely.
3. For the best flavor, add the zest to your soup at the last minute.

Juice of 1 lime/orange/lemon

1. Once you get the zest removed, roll the citrus fruit on your cutting board, pressing it down firmly with the palm of your hand to loosen up the flesh inside.
2. Cut the citrus fruit in half crosswise and squeeze out all the juice into a small bowl. Use a citrus reamer to get every last drop.
3. Pick out any seeds, or strain the juice through a sieve.
4. For the best flavor, add the juice to your soup at the last minute.

Sautéing Vegetables

If the goal of sautéing is to brown a vegetable, it is really important to preheat your pot or pan before anything goes into it. When the pot is hot, add the oil and let the oil heat before adding the vegetable that needs to be browned.

If the goal of sautéing is to cook something until it is translucent or softened, simply add the vegetable(s) along with the oil or butter, then cook over a lower temperature to avoid browning.

Browning meat

1. It's really important to preheat your pot or pan over medium-high heat for at least 2 minutes before browning meat.
2. Pat the meat well with paper towel to ensure the meat is very dry.
3. When the pot is hot, add the oil then place the pieces of meat in the pot, giving the pieces space to breathe in between.
4. If not all the meat fits in the pot, cook it in batches.
5. Don't fuss with the meat. Leave it in one place or it will never brown underneath. Only once the bottom is brown should you flip the meat over and cook it on the other side.
6. Remove the browned meat and continue cooking the remaining meat, adding more oil as needed.

Soaking and precooking beans

Soaking dried beans doesn't require much effort, but it does take some preplanning.

1. Rinse the dried beans in a few changes of cold water.
2. Place the beans in a large wide-mouth glass jar or large bowl. Fill to the top with cold water and leave in the fridge overnight.
3. The next day, drain the beans and place in a pot of cold water (water should cover the beans by at least an inch/2.5 cm). Bring to a boil and let simmer for 30 minutes or until they're tender. Drain well.

If all you have are dried beans and you need to use them right away, here is a great little shortcut.

1. Rinse the dried beans in a few changes of cold water.
2. Place a large pot over high heat. Add the beans and cover them with plenty of cold water.
3. Bring the water to a boil, then immediately drain it off.
4. Cover the beans with cold water again. Bring to a boil and drain.
5. One more time with the cold water. Bring to a boil and drain.
6. Last time with the cold water but this time, let the beans simmer for 30 minutes or until they're tender. Drain well.

Puréeing soup in a countertop blender

Warning: This is a tricky move and requires careful attention to pull it off without splattering your kitchen with soup.

1. Remove the center cap from the blender lid. This is to let the steam escape. An airtight lid combined with steam pressure and a whirling propeller is set to make a messy explosion that will leave you and your kitchen covered in dangerously hot soup.
2. Fill your blender only halfway with equal parts chunks and liquid.
3. Place the lid on the blender and place a folded dry dishcloth over the hole where the center cap was so that nothing will splatter out. You can quite safely place your hand on the cloth to hold the lid while you're puréeing the soup.
4. Start the blender on low speed and slowly bring it up to full tilt.
5. Blend until the soup is hyper-smooth, then pour it into a clean pot.
6. Continue blending the soup in small batches until it is all silky smooth.
7. To make sure your soup is as smooth as possible, pour it into the clean pot through a fine-mesh sieve to catch any last chunks.

Puréeing soup with an immersion blender

1. Place the end of the immersion blender into the soup, right to the bottom of the pot, then turn it on.
2. Move the immersion blender around the bottom of the pot to ensure there are no splatters.
3. You can even tilt the pot and work the blender around in the deep end.
4. When you think it's smooth enough, keep going for 5 more minutes so it gets even smoother.

Chilling and storing soup and stock

It's very important to know how to store hot soup and stock properly. If you simply put a big pot of hot soup in your fridge or freezer, the soup will warm up everything in your fridge or freezer and cause other foods to spoil. This is not so nice and also potentially dangerous.

To chill a big pot of soup or stock, you'll need lots of ice.

1. Put the plug in a clean kitchen sink. Place your pot of hot soup in the sink. Add ice to the sink to come one-quarter of the way up the side of the pot. If it's winter, and it might be if you're making soup, you can use freshly fallen snow instead of ice.
2. Fill the sink with cold water from the tap until it reaches the same level as the soup in the pot. Keep stirring the soup, preferably stirring in the same direction (if you do this, the soup cools faster for some reason), until the soup cools down to about lukewarm or body temperature.
3. Transfer the soup to smaller containers and store them in the fridge or freezer.

If you want to freeze a soup containing cream and/or pasta, prepare the soup without these ingredients, then freeze the soup. After thawing the soup, add the cream and/or pasta and continue with the recipe.

Stock Portfolio

Homemade stock is the secret to making the most homemade-iest of soups. With a little bit more effort, you can include completely from-scratch soups in your repertoire. Creating a stock portfolio is a great way to diversify your soup offerings. Fix a variety of stocks when you have time and then keep them in your freezer—you'll be ready to simmer up delicious, from-scratch soup whenever you feel like it!

First off, a little information on two essential building blocks of any great homemade stock.

MIREPOIX

A mirepoix is a mixture of diced vegetables used to flavor soups, sauces and stews. A classic mirepoix includes diced carrot, onion and celery, but you can also include parsnip, leek greens, shallots, mushroom, sweet pepper and asparagus, and even bacon. The classic combo was created by a chef who worked for Charles-Pierre-Gaston-François de Lévis, duke of Lévis-Mirepoix in France. It seems a shame no one knows the chef's name since he was the fellow who invented it.

BOUQUET GARNI

A bouquet garni is a lovely little bundle of herbs and spices that lends a real aroma to your stock. Your bouquet can be nicely tied in a little cheesecloth bundle or stuffed into a large tea ball, or it doesn't even have to be bundled at all, the ingredients left to float freely in the stock.

A traditional bouquet garni includes garlic, thyme, parsley stems, bay leaves, peppercorns and whole cloves. But you can also include things like rosemary, tarragon, a chunk of fresh ginger and whole cardamom pods.

Classic Comforting Stock

Makes about 6 quarts (6 L)

6 quarts (6 L) cold water
5 lb (2.2 kg) chicken bones or 8 lb (3.5 kg) beef bones

Mirepoix
1 carrot, peeled and diced
1 onion, peeled and diced
1 stalk celery, diced

Bouquet Garni
2 cloves garlic
3 sprigs parsley
2 bay leaves
1 sprig thyme
10 whole black peppercorns
2 whole cloves

1. Place the water, bones, mirepoix and bouquet garni in a large pot. The water should cover everything in the pot. If it doesn't, add more water until everything is submerged.
2. Bring to a boil, uncovered, over high heat. At the very moment you see any bubbles break the surface of the water, reduce the heat down to a bare simmer.
3. Simmer, uncovered, for 2 hours, never letting the stock boil. Boiling will cause the proteins to coagulate and come out of the bones and will result in a cloudy stock. If the boiling gets away from you, though, and you do end up with a cloudy stock, feel free to still use it. Cloudy stocks are not the end of the world—they're just not as pretty as clear stocks.
4. While the stock simmers ever so gently, use a large metal spoon to skim away any impurities that float to the surface.
5. Strain the stock by ladling it through a fine-mesh sieve lined with cheesecloth into a large bowl or a clean pot. Discard the solids and use the stock immediately, or freeze it in small containers for future use (see page 21).

Brown Stock
To add depth of flavor and color to your stock, take the bones, carrots and onions from the Classic Comforting Stock recipe, spread them out in a large roasting pan and roast them in a 450°F (230°C) oven for about 45 minutes or until they are very dark brown.

Good proper stock is something you should make from scratch at least once, so you can discover just how easy it is and how much better it tastes than store-bought stock or stock cubes. Once you've tried it, you won't want to go back!

You can use raw chicken bones (from chicken portions you've boned out) or cooked chicken bones (from the Sunday roast). Or, buy meaty beef bones (preferably those that contain marrow) from your butcher.

Fish Stock

Makes about 6 quarts (6 L)

6 quarts (6 L) cold water
5 lb (2.2 kg) fish bones or fresh fish heads (gills removed)

Mirepoix
1 carrot, peeled and diced
1 onion, peeled and diced
1 stalk celery, diced

Bouquet Garni
2 cloves garlic
3 sprigs parsley
2 bay leaves
1 sprig fresh thyme
10 whole black peppercorns

This is one stock you want to make fresh and use right away. Frozen fish stock from the store or even frozen homemade isn't all that great, so make it fresh and use it immediately. The good news: it takes way less time than meat stock.

If you don't have fish bones and heads on hand (and who does?!), buy them from your fish store. Avoid using bones and heads from oily fish (like salmon and mackerel) as these will make your stock cloudy.

1. Place the water, bones, mirepoix and bouquet garni in a large pot. The water should cover everything in the pot. If it doesn't, add more water until everything is submerged.
2. Bring to a boil, uncovered, over high heat. At the very moment you see any bubbles break the surface of the water, reduce the heat down to a bare simmer.
3. Simmer, uncovered, for 20 to 30 minutes, never letting the stock boil. Boiling will cause the proteins to coagulate and come out of the bones and will result in a cloudy stock. If the boiling gets away from you, though, and you do end up with a cloudy stock, feel free to still use it. Cloudy stocks are not the end of the world—they're just not as pretty as clear stocks.
4. While the stock simmers ever so gently, use a large metal spoon to skim away any impurities that float to the surface.
5. Strain the stock by ladling it through a fine-mesh sieve lined with cheesecloth into a large bowl or a clean pot. Discard the solids and use the stock immediately.

Simple Vegetable Stock

Makes about 6 quarts (6 L)

6 quarts (6 L) cold water

Mirepoix
2 carrots, peeled and diced
2 onions, diced
2 stalks celery, diced

Bouquet Garni
2 cloves garlic
3 sprigs parsley
1 sprig fresh thyme
2 bay leaves
10 whole black peppercorns

1. Place the water, mirepoix and bouquet garni in a large pot. The water should cover everything in the pot. If it doesn't, add more water until everything is submerged.
2. Bring to a boil, uncovered, over high heat. When the water boils, reduce the heat to medium.
3. Boil gently for 1 hour, never letting the stock boil vigorously. But, unlike with meat and fish stocks, you can still boil vegetable stock quite rapidly because there are no proteins to make the stock cloudy. So you'll be done much more quickly.
4. Strain the stock by ladling it through a fine-mesh sieve into a large bowl or a clean pot. Discard the solids and use the stock immediately, or freeze it in small containers for future use (see page 21).

Vegetable stocks are handy to have tucked away in the freezer because making vegetarian soups then becomes a cinch, and the stock's light flavor won't overwhelm whatever ingredients you add to the soup.

The SOUPS of FALL

It's no accident that we're beginning our year of scrumptious soups with fall. As the days shorten and the evenings turn chilly, we not only pack away our T-shirts and think about pulling on a sweater but also start craving heartier fare. A steaming bowl of hot soup warms the heart and can make us feel that all is right with the world.

In this chapter, you'll find soups featuring the best of fall's harvest, with recipes starring pumpkin, squash and mushrooms, apples, pears and chestnuts. There are soups to serve at Thanksgiving and Halloween, and others to make just because you feel like warming up from the inside out.

It's time to dust off your stockpot and get simmering!

Okanagan Orchard

Jennifer Schell
Soup Sister and Food Writer

vegetarian

Makes about 6 servings

1 head celeriac, peeled and diced
2 Okanagan Ambrosia apples, peeled, cored and diced
1 onion, diced
10 fresh sage leaves
5 sprigs fresh thyme, leaves only
2 Tbsp (30 mL) olive oil
6 cups (1.5 L) chicken or vegetable stock
Salt to taste
Blue cheese crostini (see below)

1. In a large pot over medium heat, sauté the celeriac, apples, onion, sage and thyme in the oil, until the onion is softened.
2. Add the stock. Bring to a boil over high heat, then reduce the heat to medium-low.
3. Simmer, uncovered, until the celeriac is tender, about 15 minutes.
4. Purée the soup until smooth. Reheat and add salt to taste.
5. Ladle up bowlfuls of the steamy, handsome soup, and float the bountifully buoyant blue cheese crostini on each one.

Blue Cheese Crostini

1. Thinly slice half a **baguette**, and bake the slices in a single layer on a baking sheet in a 350°F (180°C) oven until dry and crispy, about 30 minutes.
2. Meanwhile, heat a little **olive oil** in a small skillet over medium-high heat. Add **fresh sage leaves** and cook for a few seconds or until crisp. Remove with a slotted spoon and drain on a paper-towel-lined plate.
3. Top each baguette slice with a smear of **soft blue cheese**, some **toasted walnuts** and the **crisp sage leaves**.

This soup is a celebration of the Okanagan's harvest season and a love letter to my orchard roots. It was important to me, as someone born and raised on an apple farm, to contribute a recipe that stars this beautiful fruit. The apple is not only nutritious and delicious—for me it symbolizes home, family and love. I've also added walnuts, sage, thyme and parsley from my own backyard.
—JENNIFER SCHELL

Mushroom and Chestnut

David Robertson
Chef and Co-owner, The Dirty Apron Cooking School and
 Delicatessen, Vancouver

Makes about 6 servings

1 small onion, diced
1 oz (30 g) dried porcini
 mushrooms, soaked in hot water
 for 20 minutes then drained
2 cloves garlic, minced or finely
 chopped, divided
2 Tbsp (30 mL) vegetable oil,
 divided
1 lb (500 g) fresh chestnuts,
 peeled (see left)

1 russet potato, peeled and diced
6 cups (1.5 L) vegetable stock
1 cup (250 mL) whipping cream
 (35% MF)
½ cup (125 mL) sliced fresh
 porcini mushrooms
1 Tbsp (15 mL) sherry vinegar
Truffle oil to taste
Salt and pepper to taste
2 sprigs fresh thyme, leaves only

To peel chestnuts, cut an X in the flat side of each nut. In a saucepan of boiling water, cook the chestnuts until the edges of the cuts start to curl, about 2 minutes. Drain well. When cool enough to handle, peel off the skins with a small, sharp knife.

1. In a large pot over medium heat, sauté the onion, soaked mushrooms and half of the garlic in 1 Tbsp (15 mL) of the oil, until the onion is softened.
2. Stir in the chestnuts and potato. Sauté for 3 minutes.
3. Add the stock and cream. Bring to a boil over high heat, then reduce the heat to medium-low.
4. Simmer, uncovered, until the chestnuts and potato are tender, about 15 minutes.
5. Meanwhile, heat a small skillet over medium-high heat. Add the remaining 1 Tbsp (15 mL) oil. Sauté the fresh mushrooms and remaining garlic until the mushrooms are golden brown and tender.
6. Add the vinegar. Simmer, scraping up any browned bits from the bottom of the skillet with a wooden spoon. Drizzle with truffle oil to taste. Set aside.
7. Purée the soup until smooth. Reheat over medium heat and add salt and pepper to taste.
8. Ladle up an earthy bowlful and top with a spoonful of the sautéed mushrooms and a bright sprinkling of fresh thyme.

Apple, Carrot and Parsnip

Nettie Cronish
Cookbook Author

Makes about 6 servings

2 leeks, white and pale green parts only, washed and sliced
2 cloves garlic, minced or finely chopped
2 Tbsp (30 mL) olive oil
4 parsnips, peeled and diced
2 carrots, peeled and diced
1 Granny Smith apple, peeled, cored and diced
6 cups (1.5 L) vegetable stock
¼ tsp (1 mL) grated nutmeg
1 cup (250 mL) whipping cream (35% MF)
½ cup (125 mL) diced smoked chicken (optional, see sidebar)
Salt and pepper to taste

1. In a large pot over medium heat, sauté the leeks and garlic in the oil, until softened.
2. Stir in the parsnips, carrots and apple.
3. Add the stock and nutmeg. Bring to a boil over high heat, then reduce the heat to medium-low.
4. Simmer, uncovered, until the parsnips are tender, about 30 minutes.
5. Purée the soup until smooth. Add the cream and smoked chicken, if using. Reheat over medium heat and add salt and pepper to taste.
6. Ladle up a steamy, creamy bowlful.

This recipe is excerpted from Everyday Flexitarian *by Nettie Cronish and Pat Crocker (Whitecap Books, 2011).*

If you can't find smoked chicken at your butcher, dice up some ham and add along with regular cooked and diced chicken breast.

Let us celebrate the parsnip! The silky texture and buttery taste of this soup make it a dish you can serve hot or cold. This recipe is about choice, whether you want to serve it to vegetarians, meat eaters or both—add to that the affordability of the ingredients, and the health and environmental benefits of a flexitarian diet.
—NETTIE CRONISH

vegetarian Puréed Cauliflower

Massimo Capra
Chef and Co-owner, Mistura and Sopra Upper Lounge, Toronto

Makes about 6 servings

1 cup (250 mL) diced onion
6 cloves garlic, minced or finely chopped
2 Tbsp (30 mL) unsalted butter
3 cups (750 mL) roughly chopped cauliflower
1 cup (250 mL) peeled and diced potatoes
4 bay leaves
6 cups (1.5 L) vegetable stock (approx.)
Mushroom croutons (see right)
½ cup (125 mL) whipping cream (35% MF)
Salt and pepper to taste

1. In a large pot over medium heat, sauté the onion and garlic in the butter, until the onion is softened.
2. Stir in the cauliflower, potatoes and bay leaves.
3. Add enough stock to just cover the cauliflower. Bring to a boil over high heat, then reduce the heat to medium-low.
4. Simmer, uncovered, for 1 hour, adding more stock as needed to keep the cauliflower submerged.
5. Meanwhile, make the mushroom croutons.
6. Remove the bay leaves. Purée the soup until smooth. Add the cream. Reheat and add salt and pepper to taste.
7. Serve a steamy, creamy bowl with some toasty mushroom croutons on top.

Mushroom Croutons

¼ cup (60 mL) dried porcini mushrooms
¼ cup (60 mL) freshly grated Parmesan cheese
2½ cups (625 mL) diced focaccia bread
¼ cup (60 mL) olive oil
Salt and pepper to taste

1. Preheat the oven to 350°F (180°C).
2. Put the dried porcini mushrooms in a coffee grinder and blitz until they turn to powder. Mix the mushroom powder with the Parmesan in a large bowl and set aside.
3. In another large bowl, toss the diced focaccia with the olive oil and salt and pepper. Spread the focaccia out in a single layer on a large baking sheet. Bake for 10 to 15 minutes or until crisp and golden.
4. Remove the focaccia from the oven and immediately add to the mushroom powder mixture. Toss well.

Spicy Jamaican Pumpkin

Christine Cushing
Cookbook Author and Host of *Fearless in the Kitchen* on OWN

Makes about 6 servings

2 Tbsp (30 mL) unsalted butter
1 Tbsp (15 mL) olive oil
2 stalks celery, diced
2 large shallots, peeled and minced
1 carrot, peeled and diced
2 green onions, sliced
2 cloves garlic, minced or finely chopped
1 lb (500 g) Caribbean pumpkin or butternut squash, peeled, seeded and chopped (about 4 cups/1 L)

4 cups (1 L) chicken stock or vegetable stock
¼ seeded and minced Scotch bonnet chili or 1 tsp (5 mL) chipotle chili powder
3 sprigs fresh thyme, leaves only
2 bay leaves
⅛ tsp (0.5 mL) ground allspice
1 cup (250 mL) unsweetened coconut milk (optional)
Juice of ½ lime
Salt and pepper to taste

1. Heat a large pot over medium-high heat. Add the butter and oil. Sauté the celery, shallots, carrot, green onions and garlic until the shallots begin to soften and brown.
2. Add the remaining ingredients, except the coconut milk, lime juice, salt and pepper.
3. Bring to a boil over high heat, then reduce the heat to medium-low.
4. Cover with a lid and simmer until the pumpkin is very tender, about 30 minutes.
5. Remove the bay leaves. Purée the soup until smooth. Add the coconut milk and lime juice. Reheat over medium heat and add salt and pepper to taste.
6. Serve up a hot and spicy bowlful.

I tasted this soup on my first trip to Jamaica years ago. Ever since, I've been trying to re-create it. Make it anytime Caribbean pumpkin is available. (It's also called Jamaican pumpkin or calabaza.) I go to Caribbean specialty stores for mine. You can also use any winter squash as a substitute, although it's not quite the same. Take it is easy on the Scotch bonnet chili; it's smokin' hot!
—CHRISTINE CUSHING

Celeriac and Cauliflower

Jenni Neidhart
Catering Director, The Cookbook Co. Cooks, Calgary

Makes about 6 servings

1 head cauliflower, cut into bite-size pieces
1 Tbsp (15 mL) olive oil
2 heads celeriac, peeled and diced
4 cups (1 L) chicken or vegetable stock
2 cloves garlic, minced or finely chopped
1 Tbsp (15 mL) finely chopped fresh thyme
3 cups (750 mL) whipping cream (35% MF)
Salt and pepper to taste

1. Preheat the oven to 400°F (200°C). Line a large rimmed baking sheet with parchment paper.
2. Toss the cauliflower in olive oil, and spread out in a single layer on the baking sheet. Roast until golden brown, about 45 minutes.
3. Place the celeriac, stock, garlic and thyme in a large pot. Bring to a boil over high heat, then reduce the heat to medium-low.
4. Simmer, uncovered, until the celeriac is tender, about 25 minutes.
5. Reserving some of the smaller florets for garnish, add the roasted cauliflower to the pot, along with the cream.
6. Purée the soup until smooth. Reheat over medium heat and add salt and pepper to taste.
7. Serve up a bowl of silky soup, and garnish with some jaunty little roast cauliflower florets.

Celeriac—aka celery root—is the bulbous root of the celery plant. It looks horrible from the outside, with dirty, bumpy skin and a gnarly disposition, but inside lies the beauty of an angel's soul: pure white, glistening flesh and a heavenly celery flavor.

vegetarian

Squash, Pear and Parsnip with Ginger

dee Hobsbawn-Smith
Cookbook Author and Poet

Makes about 8 servings

4 carrots, peeled and diced
4 parsnips, peeled and diced
1 leek, white and pale green parts only, washed and sliced
1 ripe pear, peeled, cored and diced
¼ cup (60 mL) grated fresh ginger
2 Tbsp (30 mL) unsalted butter
2 medium butternut squash, peeled, seeded and diced

½ cup (125 mL) dry white wine
1 tsp (5 mL) dried oregano
6 cups (1.5 L) chicken or vegetable stock
Maple-butter croutons (see below)
Juice of 2 oranges
Juice of ½ lemon
¼ cup (60 mL) runny honey
Tabasco or other hot sauce to taste
Salt to taste
Splash of whipping cream to taste

You can purée this soup to a smooth and velvety texture or serve it in its chunky state. For best flavor, make the soup in advance and give it a day—or several—in the fridge to mature.

1. In a large pot over medium heat, sauté the carrots, parsnips, leek, pear and ginger in the butter, until the leek is softened.
2. Stir in the squash, wine and oregano.
3. Add the stock. Bring to a boil over high heat, then reduce the heat to medium-low.
4. Simmer, uncovered, until the squash is tender, about 30 minutes.
5. While the soup simmers, make the maple-butter croutons.
6. Purée the soup until smooth. Add the orange and lemon juice, honey, and Tabasco sauce to taste. Reheat over medium heat and add salt to taste.
7. Ladle up a big ol' bowl of hot soup, and add a cheeky swirl of whipping cream and some crunchy, sweet croutons.

Maple-Butter Croutons

Sauté **diced bread** in lots of **butter** until crisp. Drizzle sparingly with **maple syrup**, and continue to cook until caramelized and browned. Let cool before serving.

Jumbo Gumbo

Marian Hanna
Soup Sister

Makes about 6 servings

1 cup (250 mL) vegetable oil
1 cup (250 mL) all-purpose flour
1 lb (500 g) andouille sausage, chopped
  (see sidebar)
2 stalks celery, diced
1 onion, diced
1 green pepper, seeded and diced

2 cloves garlic, minced or finely chopped
6 cups (1.5 L) chicken stock
1 bay leaf
1 cooked whole chicken, meat shredded
  and bones and skin discarded
Creole seasoning to taste (see below)
Salt and pepper to taste

1. Heat a large pot over medium heat. Add the oil. When it begins to heat up and look swirly, gradually whisk in the flour.
2. Cook, stirring constantly, until the roux becomes the color of chocolate milk, about 3 minutes. Watch that it doesn't burn; if it does, you must discard it and start over!
3. Add the sausage, celery, onion, green pepper and garlic to the pot. Sauté until the onion is softened and the sausage is half-cooked, about 5 minutes.
4. Add the stock and bay leaf. Bring to a boil over high heat, then reduce the heat to medium-low. Simmer, uncovered, until the vegetables are tender, about 1 hour.
5. Remove the bay leaf. Add the chicken meat, Creole seasoning and salt and pepper.
6. Ladle up a bubbly, spicy bowl.

Creole Seasoning
Makes about 1 cup (250 mL)

5 Tbsp (75 mL) sweet Hungarian paprika
3 Tbsp (45 mL) kosher salt or sea salt
2 Tbsp (30 mL) dried basil leaves
2 Tbsp (30 mL) garlic powder
2 Tbsp (30 mL) onion powder

1 Tbsp (15 mL) dried thyme leaves
1 Tbsp (15 mL) dried oregano leaves
1 Tbsp (15 mL) cayenne
1 Tbsp (15 mL) ground white pepper

Stir together all the ingredients and store in an airtight container.

Andouille sausage is a spicy smoked pork sausage popular in Louisiana, where andouille features heavily in Cajun cuisine. Look for it at the best butcher store in town.

Creole seasoning can be stored in a cool, dark place for up to six months. Use it to season breaded chicken or fish, or sprinkle it over any meat you're planning to barbecue.

Mixed Mushroom

vegetarian

gluten free

Michael Bonacini
Chef and Partner, Oliver and Bonacini Restaurants, Toronto

Makes about 4 servings

¼ cup (60 mL) diced onion
2 cloves garlic, minced or finely chopped
2 Tbsp (30 mL) vegetable oil
2½ cups (625 mL) sliced assorted fresh mushrooms
1 Tbsp (15 mL) finely chopped fresh thyme
½ cup (125 mL) whipping cream (35% MF)
Salt and pepper to taste

1. In a large pot over medium heat, sauté the onion and garlic in the oil, until the onion is softened.
2. Add the mushrooms and thyme. Sauté until the mushrooms are browned.
3. Add 4 cups (1 L) water. Bring to a boil over high heat, then reduce the heat to medium-low.
4. Simmer, uncovered, until the mushrooms are tender, about 15 minutes.
5. Purée the soup until smooth. Add the cream. Reheat over medium heat and add salt and pepper to taste.
6. Ladle up a piping potage of gorgeous, mushroomy goodness.

Adding whipping cream to this soup makes it rich, creamy and velvety smooth. The soup can also be used as a sauce to accompany grilled chicken or salmon.

Curried Sweet Potato, Carrot and Red Lentil

Julie Van Rosendaal
Cookbook Author and Blogger, dinnerwithjulie.com

Makes about 4 servings

1 onion, diced
2 cloves garlic, crushed
1 Tbsp (15 mL) grated fresh ginger
1 Tbsp (15 mL) canola oil
2 carrots, peeled and diced
1 sweet potato, peeled and diced
½ cup (125 mL) red lentils, rinsed
1 tsp (5 mL) curry powder, or more to taste
4 cups (1 L) chicken or vegetable stock
½ cup (125 mL) plain yogurt or whipping cream (35% MF)
Salt to taste

1. In a large pot over medium heat, sauté the onion, garlic and ginger in the oil, until the onion is softened.
2. Stir in the carrots, sweet potato, lentils and curry powder.
3. Add the stock and 1 cup (250 mL) water. Bring to a boil over high heat, then reduce the heat to medium-low.
4. Simmer, uncovered, until the lentils are tender, about 35 minutes.
5. Purée until smooth. Add the yogurt. Reheat over medium heat (without boiling), and add salt to taste.
6. Ladle up a bubbly bowl of sweet lentil soup.

This smooth soup is mellow and slightly sweet, with a bit of spice. It is delicious to sip out of a to-go cup in the car or at my desk. I recently made a vegan version, using vegetable stock and coconut milk, to feed some sci-fi celebrities at the Calgary Entertainment Expo—Batman and Darth Vader particularly liked it. —JULIE VAN ROSENDAAL

Salt Fish and Fennel

Colin Penttinen
Chef, JAROblue, Calgary

Makes about 8 servings

1 lb (500 g) boneless, skinless halibut fillets, sliced into ½-inch
  (1 cm) strips
1 cup (250 mL) coarse salt

3 stalks celery, diced
2 fennel bulbs, trimmed and diced
1 onion, diced
1 parsnip, peeled and diced
1 leek, white and pale green parts only, washed and diced
½ cup (125 mL) olive oil
2 Tbsp (30 mL) minced or finely chopped garlic
2 Tbsp (30 mL) grated fresh ginger
4 cups (1 L) peeled and diced potatoes
2 cups (500 mL) white wine
3 quarts (3 L) chicken stock
2 Tbsp (30 mL) sherry vinegar
Salt to taste
Pickled red onion (see right)

Fennel's mild anise flavor is magical and a divine match with fish. This soup uses the fresh bulb, but you will find fennel showing up in recipes as seeds or even as pollen, adding its subtle hint of black licorice to dishes.

1. For the salt fish, combine the fish with the salt in a large bowl.
2. Lay out the strips of fish on a parchment-paper-lined baking sheet. Refrigerate, uncovered, for at least 2 hours. It can be left in the fridge for up to 2 days, although it may start to stink up the fridge a bit.
3. For the soup, sauté the celery, fennel, onion, parsnip and leek in the oil over medium heat, until the onion is softened. Be sure not to let any of the vegetables brown. Stir in the garlic and ginger.
4. Add the white wine. Bring to a boil over high heat, then reduce the heat to medium-low.

5. Add the potatoes and stock and bring to a boil over high heat. Simmer, uncovered, until the potatoes are tender.
6. Purée the soup until smooth. Return the soup to a clean pot.
7. Remove your fish from the fridge. Rinse off any excess salt and tear the fish into tiny pieces with your fingers.
8. Add the fish to the pot and simmer over low heat for 15 minutes.
9. Add the vinegar, and the salt to taste.
10. Serve up the thick and creamy soup, and garnish with a bright scattering of pickled red onion.

Pickled Red Onion
  1 red onion, thinly sliced
  1 cup (250 mL) rice vinegar

Combine the red onion, rice vinegar and 1 cup (250 mL) water in a nonreactive container. Let sit at room temperature for at least 30 minutes. The pickled onion will keep for up to 2 weeks in the fridge.

Tuscan Bean

vegan

Caren McSherry

Cookbook Author and Owner, The Gourmet Warehouse, Vancouver

Makes about 6 servings

- 2 cups (500 mL) cooked white navy beans (drained and rinsed if canned)
- 1 onion, diced
- 1 carrot, peeled and diced
- 2 stalks celery, diced
- 1 leek, white and pale green parts only, washed and sliced
- ⅓ cup (80 mL) olive oil
- 6 large Roma tomatoes, diced
- 3 cloves garlic, minced or finely chopped
- 2 sprigs fresh thyme, leaves only
- 8 cups (2 L) chicken or vegetable stock
- Salt and pepper to taste
- Sun-dried tomato crostini (see below)
- Freshly grated Parmesan cheese for garnish

1. Purée half the beans until smooth, adding a little water if necessary. Place the puréed beans in a bowl with the remaining whole beans and set aside.
2. In a large pot over medium heat, sauté the onion, carrot, celery and leek in the oil, until the onion is softened.
3. Stir in all the beans and the tomatoes, garlic and thyme.
4. Add the stock. Bring to a boil over high heat, then reduce the heat to medium-low.
5. Simmer, uncovered, until the vegetables are tender, about 30 minutes. While the pot simmers, prepare the crostini (see below).
6. Season the soup with salt and pepper to taste.
7. Ladle up in a wide shallow bowl, and garnish with grated Parmesan and playful floating crostini.

Sun-Dried Tomato Crostini
1. Thinly slice half a **baguette** and bake the slices in a single layer on a baking sheet in a 350°F (180°C) oven until dry and crispy, about 30 minutes.
2. In a small bowl combine ½ cup (125 mL) finely diced **sun-dried tomatoes** and half a bunch of **parsley**, finely minced. Spoon the mixture sparingly onto the baguette slices.

Thai Coconut Squash

Darren Nixon
Chef/Owner, Divine, Okotoks, Alberta

Makes about 8 servings

2 onions, diced
4 cloves garlic, minced or finely chopped
1 Tbsp (15 mL) grated fresh ginger
2 Tbsp (30 mL) olive oil
5 cups (1.25 L) peeled, seeded and diced butternut squash
5 stalks celery, diced
⅓ cup (80 mL) fish sauce
¼ cup (60 mL) packed brown sugar
1 Tbsp (15 mL) sambal oelek (hot chili sauce)
6 lime leaves
3 quarts (3 L) chicken stock
2 cans (14 oz/398 mL each) unsweetened coconut milk
Zest and juice of 2 limes
Salt to taste
1 bunch cilantro, roughly chopped

1. In a large pot over medium heat, sauté the onions, garlic and ginger in the oil, until the onions are softened.
2. Stir in the squash, celery, fish sauce, brown sugar, sambal oelek and lime leaves.
3. Add the stock. Bring to a boil over high heat, then reduce the heat to medium-low.
4. Simmer, uncovered, until the squash is tender, about 30 minutes.
5. Purée the soup until smooth. Add the coconut milk, and the zest and juice of the limes. Reheat over medium heat and add salt to taste.
6. Ladle up a steamy dish of soup, and garnish with a bright sprinkle of fresh cilantro.

Easy Black Bean

Bonny Babbins
Soup Sister

vegan

gluten free

Makes about 6 servings

3 carrots, peeled and diced
3 stalks celery, diced
1 onion, diced
1 Tbsp (15 mL) olive oil
1 can (19 oz/540 mL) black beans, drained and rinsed
2 cloves garlic, crushed
1 tsp (5 mL) dried basil leaves
1 tsp (5 mL) ground cumin
½ tsp (2 mL) red chili flakes
6 cups (1.5 L) chicken or vegetable stock
Salt and pepper to taste

1. In a large pot over medium heat, sauté the carrots, celery and onion in the oil, until the onion is softened.
2. Stir in the beans, garlic, basil, cumin and red chili flakes.
3. Add the stock. Bring to a boil over high heat, then reduce the heat to medium-low.
4. Simmer, uncovered, until the vegetables are tender, about 10 minutes.
5. Purée the soup until smooth. Reheat over medium heat and add salt and pepper to taste.
6. Ladle up a piping dish.

Add zip to this soup by sprinkling in as much hot sauce as you can handle, then cool things off by topping the soup with some refreshing plain yogurt.

Lily's Jewish Penicillin

Lily Lister
Soup Sister

Makes about 8 servings

1 bunch celery leaves, divided
1 bunch parsley, divided
1 bunch dill, divided
2 to 4 lb (1 to 1.8 kg) whole chicken or chicken pieces
2 chicken necks or backs
3 stalks celery, diced
3 carrots, peeled and diced
3 parsnips, peeled and diced
2 leeks, white and pale green parts only, washed and sliced
1 onion, diced
1 fennel bulb, trimmed and diced
2 Tbsp (30 mL) kosher salt or sea salt
2 bay leaves
10 whole black peppercorns
Skinny egg noodles (optional)
¼ cup (60 mL) chicken bouillon powder
1 tsp (5 mL) granulated sugar (optional)
Salt and pepper to taste

1. Line the base of a large pot with half of the celery leaves, parsley and dill. Place the whole chicken (or chicken pieces) and chicken necks on top.
2. Add 10 cups (2.5 L) water. Bring to a boil over high heat. Skim off any foam that rises to the surface. Bring to a boil and skim again.
3. Add the celery, carrots, parsnips, leeks, onion, fennel, 2 Tbsp (30 mL) salt, bay leaves and peppercorns. Bring to a boil over high heat, then reduce the heat to medium-low. Simmer, uncovered, for about 2 hours.

This is a modified version of my mother Florence's chicken soup into which she put "a little bit of this" and "a little bit of that." The fragrant, golden, magical elixir is pure solace on a cold day, and the proven remedy for a cold, sore throat, stomach ache and even a broken heart.
—LILY LISTER

4. Strain the soup into a clean pot, discarding the chicken necks, herbs and peppercorns. Set the chicken aside until it is cool enough to handle. Return the vegetables to the pot.
5. Remove the breast meat from the chicken, discarding the skin and bones. Chop the breast meat and add to the soup.
6. Finely chop the remaining celery leaves, parsley and dill. Add the celery leaves, parsley and all but 2 Tbsp (30 mL) of the dill to the soup.
7. Bring to a simmer over medium-high heat. Add the noodles (if using) and simmer until tender.
8. Gradually add the chicken bouillon to taste. Stir in the sugar (if using) and more salt and pepper to taste.
9. Ladle up a satisfying chunky bowlful and scatter with the remaining feathery dill.

Some Chicken Soup Secrets

- Always use a fresh chicken (kosher, if possible) that's neither too young nor too fatty. You can use a whole chicken, but chicken parts work well, too.
- As for vegetables, the more, the better. Sometimes I go for celery root and turnip.
- For herbs and spices, salt and pepper are mandatory. Thyme, rosemary, bay leaves, and even garlic cloves are nice additions.
- No matter how good the chicken, you will need to enhance the flavor with chicken bouillon. If you want to keep it kosher, use Osem brand bouillon.

Acorn Squash and Lentil

Susan Lobell
Soup Sister

Makes about 6 servings

4 medium acorn squash
1 onion, diced
1 carrot, peeled and diced
1 stalk celery, diced
1 Tbsp (15 mL) unsalted butter
6 cups (1.5 L) chicken or vegetable stock
2 cups (500 mL) green lentils, rinsed
1 tsp (5 mL) dried thyme leaves
Salt and pepper to taste

Crusty bread served warm and torn by hand makes the perfect dipper for this hearty autumn warmer.

1. Preheat the oven to 400°F (200°C). Line a large baking sheet with parchment paper.
2. Cut the acorn squash in half and scoop out the seeds. Place the squash, flat side down, on the baking sheet. Roast the squash until tender, about 1 hour. Remove the squash from the oven and set aside.
3. In a large pot over medium heat, sauté the onion, carrot and celery in the butter until the onion is softened.
4. Add the stock, lentils and thyme. Bring to a boil over high heat, then reduce heat to low.
5. Simmer, uncovered, until the lentils are tender, about 1 hour.
6. Scoop out bite-size pieces of roasted squash, discarding the skins. Add the squash to the pot, along with salt and pepper to taste. Heat the soup until it returns to a simmer.
7. Ladle up a bubbly handsome cup or bowl.

Comforting Fish Chowder

Laura Martin
Soup Sister

Makes about 6 servings

2 potatoes, peeled and diced
2 carrots, peeled and diced
1 onion, diced
2 cloves garlic, minced or finely chopped
2 stalks celery, diced
1½ lb (750 g) skinless cod fillets, bones removed
2 cans (12 oz/370 mL each) evaporated milk
½ cup (125 mL) milk
2 Tbsp (30 mL) sour cream
1 tsp (5 mL) granulated sugar
Salt and pepper to taste
2 Tbsp (30 mL) finely chopped parsley

1. Pile the potatoes, carrots, onion and garlic into a large pot.
2. Add enough water to just cover the ingredients. Bring to a boil over high heat, then reduce the heat to medium-low.
3. Simmer, uncovered, just until the potatoes are tender, about 20 minutes.
4. Stir in the celery. Arrange the cod on top of the vegetables. Cover the pot and steam until the celery is a little crunchy and the cod is cooked, about 5 minutes.
5. Add the evaporated milk, regular milk, sour cream and sugar. Heat over low heat. Add salt and pepper to taste.
6. Ladle up a piping vessel, and garnish with a beautiful scattering of bright green parsley.

In the last months of my mother's life, her friends expressed their love and concern by delivering delicious homemade soups to our home every couple of days. Each day, I would set a tray with the soup, a few crackers and a bud vase with a fragrant flower (and a tray with soup for myself as well), and sit by her bedside. And we would sample a new delicious soup and taste the love in every spoonful. This was one of our favorites.
—*Laura Martin*

Keith's Turkey

Rennie Hapton
Soup Sister

Makes about 6 servings

1 leftover roast turkey carcass
2 carrots, peeled and diced
2 stalks celery, diced
2 small parsnips, peeled and diced
1 onion, diced
¾ cup (185 mL) pot barley
2 to 3 bay leaves
Salt and pepper to taste

Parsnips are not pale carrots. Parsnips are much sweeter and have an amazing creamy richness that carrots cannot beat.

1. Place the turkey carcass in a large pot and add enough water to cover it completely. Bring to a boil over high heat, then reduce the heat to medium-low.
2. Simmer, uncovered, for 3 hours.
3. Pour the contents of the pot through a fine-mesh sieve. Remove any remaining turkey meat from the bones, discarding the bones and any skin. Cover and refrigerate the meat. Cover and refrigerate the stock overnight.
4. The next day, remove the fat from the surface of the stock. Pour the stock into a large pot and reheat over medium heat.
5. Add the reserved turkey meat into the stock, along with the carrots, celery, parsnips, onion, barley and bay leaves.
6. Simmer, uncovered, until the barley is tender, about 40 minutes. Remove the bay leaves. Add salt and pepper to taste.
7. Enjoy a steaming bowlful. Add a salad on the side, and you have a full meal!

Chili Blanco

Natalie Stuber
Soup Sister

Makes about 6 servings

2 onions, diced
1½ cups (375 mL) drained and diced canned green chilies
  (see sidebar)
4 cloves garlic, minced or finely chopped
¼ cup (60 mL) unsalted butter
1 Tbsp (15 mL) ground cumin
1 Tbsp (15 mL) dried oregano leaves
Salt and pepper to taste
2 cans (19 oz/540 mL each) white navy beans, drained and rinsed
2 skinless, boneless chicken breasts, diced
5 cups (1.25 L) chicken stock
½ cup (125 mL) sour cream
½ cup (125 mL) shredded white cheddar cheese
½ bunch cilantro, roughly chopped
2 limes, cut into wedges

1. In a large pot over medium heat, sauté the onions, chilies and garlic in the butter, until the onions are softened.
2. Stir in the cumin, oregano, and salt and pepper to taste.
3. Stir in the beans and chicken.
4. Add the stock. Bring to a boil over high heat, then reduce the heat to medium-low.
5. Simmer, uncovered, until the chicken is cooked through, about 15 minutes. Add more salt and pepper to taste if necessary.
6. Ladle up a white-hot cup of chili, and garnish with a plop of sour cream, some shredded white cheddar, a cheeky scattering of cilantro and lime wedges on the side.

Canned green chilies are fairly mild, and with the sour cream and cheddar around to cut the heat, this bowl of chili should appeal to everyone. But if you're worried about the amount of heat, you can tone it down by adding less canned chilies and substituting them with some green pepper.

Chicken Creole with Ancient Grains

Carolyn Sainchuck
Soup Sister

Makes about 6 servings

2 Tbsp (30 mL) vegetable oil
5 slices bacon, diced
3 skinless, boneless chicken breasts, diced
3 onions, diced
4 stalks celery, diced
1 green pepper, seeded and diced
¾ cup (185 mL) ancient grains/ rice mix (see sidebar)
4 cloves garlic, minced or finely chopped

1 tsp (5 mL) dried thyme leaves
1 tsp (5 mL) chili powder
2 bay leaves
8 cups (2 L) chicken stock
1 can (28 oz/796 mL) diced tomatoes
1 tsp (5 mL) Tabasco or other hot sauce
1 tsp (5 mL) Worcestershire sauce
Salt and pepper to taste

1. Heat a large pot over medium heat. Add the oil. Sauté the bacon until it is crispy. Remove the bacon with a slotted spoon and drain on a paper-towel-lined plate.
2. Sauté the chicken, onions, celery and green pepper in the bacon fat remaining in the pot until the onions are softened.
3. Stir in the ancient grains mix, garlic, thyme, chili powder and bay leaves.
4. Add the stock and tomatoes with their juice. Bring to a boil over high heat, then reduce the heat to medium-low.
5. Simmer, uncovered, until the grains are tender, about 35 minutes.
6. Remove the bay leaves. Stir in the Tabasco and Worcestershire sauces, and add salt and pepper to taste.
7. Ladle up a hearty cup of chunky soup garnished with bacon bits.

Our favorite mix of ancient grains and rice includes medium-grain red rice, Himalayan long-grain red rice, hull-less barley, black barley, rye berries, whole oats and quinoa, but feel free to pick your favorite mix, or come up with your own combo.

vegetarian West Indian Pumpkin

Liz Fitzhenry
Soup Sister

Makes about 4 servings

1 onion, diced
¼ cup (60 mL) unsalted butter
2 cups (500 mL) peeled, seeded and diced
   Caribbean pumpkin (aka Jamaican pumpkin,
   calabaza) or butternut squash
1 tsp (5 mL) hot curry powder
½ tsp (2 mL) ground Jamaican allspice
4 cups (1 L) chicken or vegetable stock
Curried croutons (see below)
¾ cup (185 mL) table cream or half-and-half
   (18% or 10% MF)
Salt and pepper to taste

1. In a large pot over medium heat, sauté the onion in the butter, until the onion is softened.
2. Stir in the pumpkin, curry powder and allspice.
3. Add the stock. Bring to a boil over high heat, then reduce the heat to medium-low.
4. Simmer, uncovered, until the pumpkin is tender, about 20 minutes.
5. While the soup simmers, prepare the curried croutons.
6. Purée the soup until smooth. Add the cream. Reheat over medium heat, and add salt and pepper to taste.
7. Ladle up a spicy bowlful and scatter with crunchy curried croutons.

Curried Croutons
½ cup (125 mL) unsalted butter
2 cups (500 mL) diced bread
1 tsp (5 mL) curry powder
Salt to taste

1. Melt the butter in a skillet over medium heat. Add the bread and toss to coat in the butter.
2. Sprinkle the curry powder and salt over the croutons from a nice dramatic height.
3. Sauté the croutons until they are lovely and toasty and golden. Just don't leave them unattended, or they'll burn.

The Madeira Ladies' Lentil

Margareth Lobo
Soup Sister

Makes about 6 servings

1½ cups (375 mL) red lentils, rinsed
1 onion, diced
2 cloves garlic, minced or finely chopped
1 Tbsp (15 mL) grated fresh ginger
Pinch of red chili flakes
2 tsp (10 mL) olive oil
1 tsp (5 mL) ghee or clarified butter
6 cups (1.5 L) chicken or vegetable stock
1 tsp (5 mL) ground cumin
½ tsp (2 mL) ground coriander
¼ tsp (1 mL) turmeric
½ lemon
Salt and pepper to taste
2 tomatoes, seeded and diced
2 Tbsp (30 mL) finely chopped cilantro
Chopped dry-cured hot chorizo (optional)

1. Wash the lentils in several changes of water until the water runs clear. Drain well and set aside.
2. In a large pot over medium heat, sauté the onion, garlic, ginger and red chili flakes in the oil and ghee, until the onion is softened.
3. Add the lentils and cook, stirring, for another 5 minutes.
4. Add the stock, cumin, coriander and turmeric. Bring to a boil over high heat, then reduce the heat to medium-low.
5. Simmer, uncovered, until the lentils are tender and the soup thickens, 20 to 30 minutes.
6. Add a squeeze of lemon juice, and salt and pepper to taste.
7. Ladle into bowls and finish with a flourish of diced tomatoes and chopped cilantro, adding chopped chorizo, if you wish.

vegetarian

gluten free

As is apparent from the list of spices, this is more like a dal curry than a soup . . . My aunty Ida gave this soup recipe to my mother. My mother changed it a bit. Then she gave it to me and I changed it a bit. Each of us claims our version is better than the one before. What can I say? It's one of our long-standing family traditions. The recipe is now with my niece, Amanda, who will likely change it for the next edition of this cookbook!
—MARGARETH LOBO

Eva's Heritage Borscht

Karen Anderson
Owner and Tour Guide, Calgary Food Tours Inc.

Makes about 6 servings

1 lb (500 g) pork side ribs
2 to 3 beets, trimmed
2 cups (500 mL) peeled and diced
  carrots
1 onion, diced
1 cup (250 mL) chopped fresh
  green beans

1 cup (250 mL) chopped cabbage
1 cup (250 mL) tomato juice
2 tsp (10 mL) apple cider vinegar
Salt and pepper to taste
1 cup (250 mL) sour cream
2 Tbsp (30 mL) finely chopped
  parsley or fresh dill

1. Put the ribs in a large pot and add enough water to cover them. Bring to a boil over high heat and skim off any gray scum that floats up.
2. Reduce the heat to low. Simmer, uncovered, until the ribs are tender, about 1 hour.
3. While the ribs are cooking, put the beets in a saucepan and add enough water to cover them. Bring to a boil over high heat. Reduce the heat to medium and simmer until tender, about 45 minutes.
4. Drain the beets. Set them aside until they are cool enough to handle. Peel and chop the beets, then set aside.
5. Remove the ribs from the pot, reserving the cooking water in the pot. Using a fork or knife, pull or cut the meat from the bones and chop into bite-size chunks. Return the pork to the pot.
6. Add the carrots, onion, green beans, cabbage, tomato juice and vinegar. Bring to a boil over high heat, then reduce the heat to medium-low.
7. Simmer, uncovered, until all the vegetables are tender, 20 to 30 minutes.
8. Add the boiled beets and salt and pepper to taste.
9. Ladle the soup into bowls, and swirl in a few spoonfuls of sour cream.

My husband's grandmother Eva immigrated to Canada from Eastern Europe. She was never sure if she was Polish or Ukrainian—their town was on the border, and the lines between countries changed so many times they lost track—but she made perogies and cabbage rolls with the deftest of Ukrainian precision! I inherited this borscht recipe from Eva—it's what my in-laws call great peasant food. The pork ribs give it substance and the deep maroon color makes finding the green beans a nice surprise. Add sour cream and a sprinkle of fresh dill, and it will satisfy your family on a crisp fall day.
—KAREN ANDERSON

Mushroom, Bean and Barley

Sharon Hapton
Soup Sister

Makes about 8 servings

½ cup (125 mL) dried wild mushrooms
2 onions, diced
2 carrots, peeled and diced
2 stalks celery, diced
2 Tbsp (30 mL) vegetable oil
4 cups (1 L) diced assorted fresh mushrooms
3 cloves garlic, minced or finely chopped
1 can (19 oz/540 mL) white kidney beans, drained and rinsed
1 cup (250 mL) pearl barley
8 cups (2 L) chicken or vegetable stock
Salt and pepper to taste
3 Tbsp (45 mL) finely chopped parsley

1. Soak the dried mushrooms in enough hot water to cover them for 30 minutes. When softened, strain the mushrooms, reserving the liquid. Rinse any grit from the mushrooms. Dice them and set aside.
2. In a large pot over medium heat, sauté the onions, carrots and celery in the oil, until the onions are softened.
3. Add the fresh and soaked mushrooms and garlic. Sauté for 10 minutes.
4. Stir in the beans and barley.
5. Add the stock and mushroom-soaking liquid. Bring to a boil over high heat, then reduce the heat to medium-low.
6. Simmer, uncovered, until the barley is tender and the soup thickens, about 30 minutes.
7. Add salt and pepper to taste.
8. Ladle up a chunky simmering cup, and garnish with an enlightening sprinkle of chopped parsley.

This recipe, from Bonnie Stern's HeartSmart *(Random House Canada, 2006), is one of my favorites. Over the years, this savory, nourishing and fulfilling soup seems to be the one I deliver most often to friends and family. Bonnie was kind enough to let me include it in this book.*

—SHARON HAPTON

Pasta e Fagioli

Andrea Nicholson
Chef/Owner, Killer Condiments, Toronto

Makes about 4 servings

⅓ cup (80 mL) diced pancetta
1 onion, diced
1 clove garlic, minced or finely chopped
1 can (19 oz/540 mL) white beans, drained and rinsed
1 can (19 oz/540 mL) tomatoes, roughly chopped
1 carrot, peeled and diced
1 stalk celery, diced
1⅔ cups (410 mL) chicken stock
⅓ cup (80 mL) small tubular pasta
2 Tbsp (30 mL) finely chopped parsley
Salt and pepper to taste
Freshly grated Parmesan cheese for garnish

1. Heat a large pot over medium heat. Sauté the pancetta until crispy.
2. Remove the pancetta with a slotted spoon and drain on a paper-towel-lined plate.
3. Sauté the onion and garlic in the fat remaining in the pot over medium heat until the onion is softened.
4. Add the beans, tomatoes, carrot, celery and stock. Bring to a boil over high heat, then reduce the heat to medium-low.
5. Simmer, uncovered, until the carrots and celery are tender, about 20 minutes.
6. Use a potato masher to mash some of the beans, releasing their starch to help thicken the soup.
7. Add the pasta and simmer, uncovered, until the pasta is tender, about 10 minutes.
8. Remove the pot from the heat and add the parsley, and salt and pepper to taste.
9. Ladle up a steamy handsome bowl, and garnish with a sprinkle of grated Parmesan and some crispy pancetta.

Don't have pancetta? Use bacon. Don't have bacon? Use prosciutto. Don't have prosciutto? Use ham. They'll all be yummy.

Dutch Meatball

Deborah Lewis
Soup Sister

Makes about 6 servings

1 lb (500 g) lean ground beef
½ cup (125 mL) dry bread crumbs
½ tsp (2 mL) each salt and pepper
¼ tsp (1 mL) grated nutmeg
3 carrots, peeled and diced
3 stalks celery, diced
3 leeks, white and pale green parts only, washed and sliced
2 Tbsp (30 mL) vegetable oil
4 cups (1 L) beef stock
1 cup (250 mL) cooked fine egg noodles
1 tsp (5 mL) Worcestershire sauce
Soy sauce to taste
2 Tbsp (30 mL) finely chopped parsley

My mother-in-law—who immigrated to Canada from Holland—frequently made her homemade meatball soup when we visited her house. It was a clear favorite amongst her grandchildren. While nothing could quite replicate her Dutch meatball soup, this version does an excellent job and reminds us all of those wonderful family lunches at Oma's house!
—DEBORAH LEWIS

1. Combine the ground beef, bread crumbs, salt, pepper and nutmeg in a bowl. Cover and refrigerate.
2. In a large pot over medium heat, sauté the carrots, celery and leeks in the oil, until the leeks are softened.
3. Add the stock and 4 cups (1 L) water. Bring to a boil over high heat.
4. While the soup comes to a boil, form the meat mixture into meatballs, and place on a plate or cutting board.
5. Reduce the heat to medium-low. Gently plunk the meatballs into the soup, adding more water, if needed, to ensure they are submerged.
6. Simmer, uncovered, until the meatballs are no longer pink inside, about 15 minutes.
7. Add the noodles and stir gently. Add the Worcestershire, and the soy sauce to taste.
8. Ladle up a bubbly lumpy bowlful of beefy meatballs, and garnish with a perky punch of parsley.

Potato and Leek

Lori Thompson
Soup Sister

vegetarian

gluten free

Makes about 4 servings

1 onion, diced
1 leek, white and pale green parts only, washed and sliced
1 clove garlic, minced or finely chopped
¼ cup (60 mL) unsalted butter
2 potatoes, peeled and diced
4 cups (1 L) chicken or vegetable stock
1 cup (250 mL) whipping cream (35% MF)
Salt and pepper to taste
3 Tbsp (45 mL) finely chopped fresh chives

1. In a large pot over medium heat, sauté the onion, leek and garlic in the butter, until the onion is softened.
2. Pile in the potatoes and add the stock. Bring to a boil over high heat, then reduce the heat to medium-low.
3. Simmer, uncovered, until the potatoes are tender, about 35 minutes.
4. Purée the soup until smooth. Add the cream. Reheat gently over medium heat and add salt and pepper to taste.
5. Ladle up a hot handsome bowl. Or, chill overnight and serve a chilly cup. Either way, garnish with bright green chives.

At warmer times of the year, this creamy potato and leek makes an excellent chilled soup, in which case you call it *vichyssoise*. It may sound like a potato milkshake, but trust the French (who came up with vichyssoise in the first place); they know a bit about cooking.

The SOUPS of WINTER

If "the weather outside is frightful," it's the very best time of year to make soup. With a big pot bubbling away on the stove, your kitchen will become a cozy haven. When family and friends tramp in, knocking the snow off their boots, you can welcome them with the comforting aroma of lovely, homemade soup.

The recipes here are undeniably hearty, and perfect for filling hungry tummies after a hockey game, an afternoon on the slopes or just a tedious, slushy commute.

Curried Squash and Coconut

Rogelio Herrera
Chef/Owner, Alloy, Calgary

Makes about 8 servings

2 large butternut squash, peeled, seeded and diced (reserve seeds for toasting)
7 cups (1.75 L) chicken or vegetable stock
4 carrots, peeled and diced
2 onions, diced
1 can (14 oz/398 mL) unsweetened coconut milk

1 Tbsp (15 mL) curry powder
1 tsp (5 mL) sweet Hungarian paprika
1 tsp (5 mL) red chili flakes
2 cups (500 mL) plain yogurt
¼ cup (60 mL) finely chopped fresh mint
¼ cup (60 mL) runny honey
Salt to taste
Toasted squash seeds (see below)

1. Combine the butternut squash, stock, carrots, onions, coconut milk, curry powder, paprika and red chili flakes in a large pot.
2. Place the pot over high heat and bring to a boil. Reduce the heat to low.
3. Simmer, uncovered, until the squash and carrots are tender, about 20 minutes.
4. Meanwhile, stir together the yogurt, mint and honey in a bowl.
5. Purée the soup until smooth. Reheat over medium heat and add salt to taste.
6. Serve a sweet, smooth bowl of soup with a bright dollop of minty yogurt and some crunchy toasted squash seeds.

Toasted Squash Seeds

When you are preparing the squash, keep the **seeds** and carefully remove the squash gunk from them. Wash and dry the seeds. Toss the clean seeds with a good drizzle of **honey** and **vegetable oil** and a big pinch of **curry powder**. Spread out the seeds in one even layer on a parchment-paper-lined baking sheet. Bake in a 350°F (180°C) oven, stirring occasionally, until the seeds are toasted, 15 to 20 minutes (watch them carefully). **Salt** liberally before serving.

Lapsang Tea, Lemon and Miso

Dan Clapson
Food Writer and Blogger, dansgoodside.com

Makes about 4 servings

4 cups (1 L) steeped *lapsang souchong* tea (see note)
2 cups (500 mL) beef or vegetable stock
3 whole cloves garlic
½ cup (125 mL) miso paste
Zest of 1 lemon
1 Tbsp (15 mL) fresh lemon juice
1 Tbsp (15 mL) grated fresh ginger
2 tsp (10 mL) wasabi paste
1 tsp (5 mL) rice wine vinegar
1 cup (250 mL) diced oyster mushrooms
1 cup (250 mL) diced soft tofu
Pepper to taste
½ cup (125 mL) finely chopped green onions

1. Combine the tea, stock and garlic in a large pot. Bring to a boil over high heat, then reduce the heat to medium-low. Simmer, uncovered, for 5 minutes.
2. Add the miso paste and stir until it has dissolved.
3. Add the lemon zest and juice, ginger, wasabi and vinegar. Simmer to blend the flavors, about 3 minutes.
4. Add the oyster mushrooms and tofu. Simmer until the mushrooms are tender, about 10 minutes. Add pepper to taste. The miso paste should be plenty salty enough, so the soup probably won't need any salt.
5. Just before serving, toss in the green onions, then serve up a comforting, steamy bowl.

Lapsang souchong tea is a smoked black tea from Fujian Province in China.

This soup totally rocks for anyone with a cold, and is great for clearing the sinuses!
—DAN CLAPSON

Potato and Bacon with Cheddar

Patrick Dunn
Chef/Owner, InterCourse Chef Services, and Instructor, The
Cookbook Co. Cooks, Calgary

Makes about 6 servings

4 slices bacon, diced
1½ cups (375 mL) washed and sliced leeks, white and pale green
  parts only
1½ lb (750 g) Yukon gold potatoes, peeled and diced
1 Tbsp (15 mL) finely chopped fresh thyme leaves
6 cups (1.5 L) chicken stock
1 cup (250 mL) shredded aged cheddar cheese
1 cup (250 mL) sour cream
Salt and pepper to taste

Play with the flavor of this soup by subbing a different firm cheese if you fancy it. Good ones to try are Emmenthal, fontina and Monterey Jack.

1. Heat a large pot over medium heat. Sauté the bacon until crispy.
2. Remove the bacon with a slotted spoon and drain on a paper-towel-lined plate.
3. Sauté the leeks in the bacon fat remaining in the pot over medium-low heat until the leeks are softened.
4. Stir in the potatoes and thyme.
5. Add the stock. Bring to a boil over high heat, then reduce the heat to medium-low.
6. Simmer, uncovered, until the potatoes are tender, about 20 minutes.
7. Remove the pot from the heat and stir in the cheddar cheese and sour cream. Add salt and pepper to taste.
8. Ladle up a chunky dish, and garnish with the crunchy bits of bacon.

Workday Irish Beef Stew

Sheila Alwell
Soup Sister

Makes about 6 servings

2 Tbsp (30 mL) olive oil
2 onions, diced
5 cloves garlic, minced or finely chopped
2½ lb (1.25 kg) bottom beef sirloin (in one piece),
   fat trimmed
3 potatoes, peeled and diced
3 carrots, peeled and diced
2 stalks celery, diced
1 Tbsp (15 mL) finely chopped fresh thyme
2 bay leaves
4 cups (1 L) beef stock
1 cup (250 mL) frozen peas, thawed and drained
Salt and pepper to taste

1. Heat a large pot over medium-high heat. Add the oil. When the oil
   is hot, sauté the onions and garlic until the onions are browned.
2. Transfer the onions and garlic to a slow cooker. Pile in the beef,
   potatoes, carrots, celery, thyme and bay leaves. Add the stock.
3. Cover and cook on low for 6 to 7 hours or until the meat is tender.
4. Remove the bay leaves. With two forks, pull the meat apart into
   chunks. Stir in the peas, and add salt and pepper to taste.
5. Ladle up a chunky, bubbly bowl of lovely Irish warmth.

If you don't have a slow
cooker, follow the same
recipe, piling everything
into the (ovenproof) pot
you used to cook the
onions. Cover the pot with
the lid and pop it into a
250°F (120°C) oven for
4 to 5 hours.

Chicken, Wild Rice and Mushroom

Carmie Nearing
Soup Sister

Makes about 10 servings

6 carrots, peeled and diced
6 stalks celery, diced
2 leeks, white and pale green parts only, washed and sliced
4 cloves garlic, minced or finely chopped
1 Tbsp (15 mL) finely chopped fresh thyme
2 Tbsp (30 mL) olive oil
1 lb (500 g) assorted fresh mushrooms (such as portobello, shiitake and cremini), sliced
4 quarts (4 L) chicken stock
4 skinless, boneless chicken breasts, diced or sliced
⅔ cup (160 mL) wild rice
⅓ cup (80 mL) brown rice
Salt and pepper to taste

If your wild rice takes ages to become tender, it could be that it's a tad stale. Buy wild rice in smallish quantities from a store with a fast turnover, so you can be sure it's fresh.

1. In a large pot over medium heat, sauté the carrots, celery, leeks, garlic and thyme in the oil, until the leeks are softened.
2. Turn up the heat to high. Add the mushrooms and sauté for 10 minutes.
3. Add the stock, chicken, wild rice and brown rice. Bring to a boil over high heat, then reduce the heat to medium-low.
4. Simmer, uncovered, until the rice is tender, 30 to 40 minutes. Add salt and pepper to taste.
5. Ladle up a steamy, chunky cup.

Oxtail Borscht

Karen Barnaby
Chef: Product Development, Albion Fisheries, Vancouver

Makes about 8 servings

5 lb (2.2 kg) oxtail pieces
1¼ lb (625 g) beets, trimmed
2 cups (500 mL) diced red cabbage
1 cup (250 mL) peeled and diced rutabaga
1 leek, white and pale green parts only, washed and sliced
½ cup (125 mL) peeled and diced parsnip
¼ cup (60 mL) peeled and diced carrot
1 lb (500 g) potatoes, peeled and diced
1 Tbsp (15 mL) caraway seeds
1 lb (500 g) Swiss chard, stems removed and leaves chopped
1 bunch dill, finely chopped
2 Tbsp (30 mL) red wine vinegar
Salt and pepper to taste
2 cups (500 mL) sour cream

1. Prepare the oxtail and the beets a day before you plan to eat the soup. Preheat the oven to 300°F (150°C). In a very large ovenproof pot, pile in the oxtail and enough water to cover the oxtail by a few inches.
2. Bring to a boil over high heat and skim off any scum that rises to the surface. Cover the pot and transfer it to the oven. Cook for 4 hours.
3. Meanwhile, place the beets on a parchment-paper-lined baking sheet and cover tightly with foil. Roast in the oven along with the pot of oxtail until the beets are tender, about 2 hours.
4. Remove the beets from the oven and set aside until cool enough to handle.
5. Holding the beets under cool, running water, peel off the loosened skin with your fingers. Cover and refrigerate the beets overnight.

I love this soup, so when I make it, I make a big batch. It's a full meal so I find it well worth the effort. You must start the soup the day before you plan to eat it, but the preparation is leisurely when stretched out over two days. The soup also freezes beautifully.

—*KAREN BARNABY*

6. When the oxtail has finished cooking, remove the pieces from the pot with a slotted spoon, and set aside until cool enough to handle. Strain the stock and refrigerate, covered, overnight.

7. Remove the meat from the oxtail bones, discarding the bones. Cover and refrigerate overnight.

8. The next day, remove the solidified fat from the surface of the stock.

9. Put the stock, beets, cabbage, rutabaga, leek, parsnip and carrot in a very large pot. Bring to a boil over high heat, then reduce the heat to medium-low.

10. Simmer, uncovered, for 30 minutes.

11. Add the potatoes and caraway seeds. Simmer for a further 15 minutes.

12. Add the oxtail meat, Swiss chard, dill and vinegar. Simmer until all the vegetables are tender and the Swiss chard has wilted, about 15 minutes. Add salt and pepper to taste.

13. Ladle up a gorgeous, meaty bowlful of chunky deliciousness and gloop a big scoop of sour cream on top.

Lamb Fagioli

Nicole Kammerer
Chef/Owner, Nicole Gourmet, Calgary

Makes about 8 servings

⅓ cup (80 mL) olive oil
1 cup (250 mL) lamb sausage
   meat, casings removed and
   meat crumbled
1 onion, diced
1 carrot, peeled and diced
3 cloves garlic, minced or finely
   chopped
2 Tbsp (30 mL) finely chopped
   fresh rosemary
1 Tbsp (15 mL) finely chopped
   fresh sage
1 tsp (5 mL) red chili flakes
1 can (28 oz/796 mL) tomatoes,
   drained

8 cups (2 L) chicken stock
2 cups (500 mL) cooked
   cannellini beans (drained and
   rinsed if canned)
¾ cup (185 mL) ditali pasta or
   other short, macaroni-type
   pasta
3 cups (750 mL) roughly
   chopped Swiss chard leaves
Salt and pepper to taste
1 cup (250 mL) freshly grated
   Parmesan cheese
2 Tbsp (30 mL) finely chopped
   parsley

1. Heat a large pot over medium-high heat. Add the oil. When the oil
    is hot, sauté the lamb sausage meat until browned.
2. Reduce the heat to medium. Add the onion, carrot, garlic,
    rosemary, sage and red chili flakes. Sauté until the carrots start
    to soften.
3. Crush the tomatoes slightly with a potato masher. Add to the pot,
    along with the stock and beans.
4. Bring to a boil over high heat. Add the pasta. Reduce the heat to
    low. Simmer, covered, for 10 minutes.
5. Add the Swiss chard. Simmer until the pasta is tender and the
    Swiss chard has wilted, about 5 minutes. Add salt and pepper
    to taste.
6. Ladle up a piping cup, and garnish with a scattering of playful
    Parmesan and punchy parsley.

Drizzling bowls of this
soup with extra virgin olive
oil adds a really lovely
fruity aroma. And if you
can find oil with some
really fresh green tones,
the drizzling also adds a
splash of great color!

Pemberton Potato

Andrea Carlson
Executive Chef, Bishop's, Vancouver

Makes about 4 servings

1 onion, diced
2 Tbsp (30 mL) unsalted butter
12 oz (375 g) Yukon gold potatoes, peeled and chopped
1 Tbsp (15 mL) finely chopped fresh thyme
1 bay leaf
2 cups (500 mL) vegetable stock
⅓ cup (80 mL) whipping cream (35% MF)
Salt to taste

The B.C. town of Pemberton, just north of Whistler, is a unique and wonderful little spot. It's located in Pemberton Valley, which produces small and particularly tasty potatoes.

1. In a large pot over medium heat, sauté the onion in the butter, until the onion is softened.
2. Stir in the potatoes, thyme and bay leaf.
3. Add the stock. If the potatoes aren't submerged, add a little water. Bring to a boil over high heat, then reduce the heat to medium-low.
4. Simmer, uncovered, until the potatoes are tender, about 20 minutes.
5. Remove the bay leaf. Purée the soup until smooth. Add the cream. Reheat over medium heat and add salt to taste.
6. Ladle up a piping cup of creamy potato potage.

Smoky Bean and Bacon

Glenys Morgan
Barbara-Jo's Books to Cooks, Vancouver

Makes about 8 servings

2 Tbsp (30 mL) vegetable oil
6 slices bacon, diced
2 onions, diced
4 carrots, peeled and diced
2 cloves garlic, crushed
3 Tbsp (45 mL) finely chopped fresh rosemary
½ tsp (2 mL) red chili flakes
8 cups (2 L) chicken stock
3 cups (750 mL) cooked fresh or frozen baby lima beans, skins
  removed
Salt and pepper to taste

1. Heat a large pot over medium-high heat. Add the oil. When the oil is hot, sauté the bacon, onions, carrots and garlic until the onions are browned.
2. Stir in the rosemary and red chili flakes.
3. Add the stock and beans. Bring to a boil over high heat, then reduce the heat to medium-low.
4. Simmer, uncovered, until the vegetables are tender, about 20 minutes.
5. Purée the soup until smooth. Reheat over medium heat and add salt and pepper to taste.
6. Ladle up a steamy smooth bowlful.

Don't be afraid of lima beans—they are delicious. If you hopped on the edamame bandwagon, you should give lima beans (and fava beans) a try, too.

vegetarian

gluten free

Butternut Squash and Apple

Lynne Oreck-Wener
Soup Sister

Makes about 4 servings

2 cups (500 mL) peeled, seeded and diced butternut squash
2 carrots, peeled and diced
2 leeks, white and pale green parts only, washed and sliced
1 onion, diced
1 potato, peeled and diced
1 tart apple (such as a Granny Smith), peeled, cored and diced
2 Tbsp (30 mL) unsalted butter
4 cups (1 L) chicken or vegetable stock
½ cup (125 mL) whipping cream (35% MF)
¼ tsp (1 mL) grated nutmeg
Salt and pepper to taste

Make sure you choose a nice tart apple like a Granny Smith. Teamed with the sweet butternut squash, an apple that's equally sweet will make this soup taste like a warm milkshake, which is not what you want at all.

1. In a large pot over medium heat, sauté the squash, carrots, leeks, onion, potato and apple in the butter, until the onion is softened.
2. Add the stock. Bring to a boil over high heat, then reduce the heat to medium-low.
3. Simmer, uncovered, until the vegetables are tender, about 25 minutes.
4. Purée the soup until smooth. Add the cream and nutmeg. Reheat over medium heat and add salt and pepper to taste.
5. Ladle up a hot, lovely bowl.

Hearty Vegetarian Bowl

vegan

Helen Swartz and Susan Finestone
Soup Sisters

Makes about 6 servings

1 onion, diced
2 cloves garlic, minced or finely chopped
2 Tbsp (30 mL) olive oil
4 cups (1 L) V8 vegetable juice
4 cups (1 L) vegetable stock
3 cups (750 mL) frozen mixed vegetables
1 can (28 oz/796 mL) tomatoes
2 pkgs (12 oz/340 g each) vegetarian ground beef
1 can (19 oz/540 mL) kidney beans, drained and rinsed
¼ head cabbage, cored and diced
1 sweet potato, peeled and diced
2 Tbsp (30 mL) balsamic vinegar
Salt and pepper to taste

1. In a large pot over medium heat, sauté the onion and garlic in the oil, until the onion is softened.
2. Pile in the remaining ingredients, except the salt and pepper. Bring to a boil over high heat, then reduce the heat to medium-low.
3. Simmer, uncovered, until the soup is thickened, about 1 hour. Add salt and pepper to taste.
4. Ladle up a chunky bunch of vegetables in a hearty party bowl.

Vegetarian ground beef (or "ground round") can be found at specialty or health food shops in the refrigerated meat-alternatives area.

Italian Lentil with Sausage

Shari Miller
Soup Sister

Makes about 4 servings

1 onion, diced
1 carrot, peeled and diced
1 stalk celery, diced
2 Tbsp (30 mL) olive oil
2 sweet or hot Italian sausages, casings removed
  and meat crumbled
1 clove garlic, minced or finely chopped
6 cups (1.5 L) chicken stock
2 tomatoes, seeded and diced
1 potato, peeled and diced
½ cup (125 mL) green lentils, rinsed
Salt and pepper to taste
¼ cup (60 mL) finely chopped parsley

1. In a large pot over medium heat, sauté the onion, carrot and celery in the oil, until the onion is softened.
2. Add the crumbled sausage meat and the garlic. Sauté until the sausage is half-cooked.
3. Add the stock, tomatoes, potato and lentils. Bring to a boil over high heat, then reduce the heat to medium-low.
4. Simmer, uncovered, until the lentils are tender, about 30 minutes. Add salt and pepper to taste.
5. Ladle up a thick and chunky bowlful, and garnish with a playful scattering of parsley.

Dress up this sausage potage with other fresh herbs, like finely shredded basil, chopped oregano or chopped chives.

Hearty Sausage Minestrone

Michal Ofer
Soup Sister

Makes about 6 servings

2 Tbsp (30 mL) olive oil

12 oz (375 g) sweet Italian sausages, casings removed and meat crumbled

8 fresh sage leaves, finely chopped

1 sprig fresh rosemary, leaves finely chopped

1 sprig fresh thyme, leaves finely chopped

3 cloves garlic, minced or finely chopped

2 carrots, peeled and diced

2 stalks celery, diced

1 onion, diced

2 cans (19 oz/540 mL each) cannellini beans, drained and rinsed

4 cups (1 L) chicken stock

1 can (28 oz/796 mL) crushed tomatoes

2 bay leaves

2 cups (500 mL) small rigatoni

Salt and pepper to taste

1 cup (250 mL) freshly grated Parmesan cheese

½ bunch parsley, finely chopped

Hearty says it all! Any leftovers are even better the next day, and the soup freezes well, too.

1. Heat a large pot over medium-high heat. Add the oil. When the oil is hot, sauté the sausage meat until browned.
2. Stir in the sage, rosemary, thyme and garlic.
3. Pile in the carrots, celery and onion. Sauté until the onion is softened.
4. Add the beans, stock, tomatoes and bay leaves. Bring to a boil over high heat, then reduce the heat to medium-low.
5. Stir in the rigatoni, bring back to a simmer and cook, uncovered, until the pasta is tender, about 15 minutes. Remove the bay leaves. Add salt and pepper to taste.
6. Ladle up a hot, chunky cup, and garnish with an enlightening flourish of Parmesan and parsley.

Weekday Hamburger

Nada Vuksic
Soup Sister

Makes about 6 servings

3 Tbsp (45 mL) vegetable oil
4 carrots, peeled and diced
1 onion, diced
½ lb (250 g) ground beef
3 stalks celery, diced
½ cup (125 mL) pot barley
4 cups (1 L) beef stock
1 can (28 oz/796 mL) diced tomatoes
1 can (28 oz/796 mL) crushed tomatoes
1 bay leaf
Salt and pepper to taste
¼ cup (60 mL) finely chopped parsley

1. Heat a large pot over medium-high heat. Add the oil. When the oil is hot, sauté the carrots and onion until the onion is browned.
2. Add the ground beef, celery and barley. Sauté until the beef is browned, breaking it into small pieces with a spatula.
3. Add the stock, diced and crushed tomatoes, bay leaf and 2 cups (500 mL) water. Bring to a boil over high heat, then reduce the heat to medium-low.
4. Simmer, covered, until the soup thickens, about 90 minutes. Remove the bay leaf. Add salt and pepper to taste.
5. Ladle up a chunky bowl, and garnish with a cheeky sprinkling of punchy parsley.

An old favorite that I make to feed a crowd, especially if they're teens and kids. I wouldn't call it glamorous, but it's definitely yummy!
—NADA VUKSIC

Cast Iron Cannellini and Kale

Connie DeSousa and John Jackson
Chefs, Charcut Roast House, Calgary

We use cast iron for cooking all braised dishes that require a low and slow heat. It has been around for centuries and will last forever if cared for properly. It's also the green choice as there are no toxic chemicals used for the non-stick surface, and you use less energy to cook.
—CONNIE DESOUSA

For us, this soup represents true comfort. The smell of garlic, sausage, wilted kale and Parmesan will make you feel warm, especially combined with the heartiness of cannellini beans and stewed tomatoes. Serve this soup family style by placing your big cast iron pot in the middle of the table: break bread, eat soup and stay warm.
—JOHN JACKSON

Makes about 6 servings

1 onion, diced
¼ cup (60 mL) olive oil
12 cloves garlic, sliced
6 cups (1.5 L) chopped kale leaves
½ lb (250 g) wine-and-cheese sausage or sweet Italian sausage, diced
½ cup (125 mL) white wine
8 cups (2 L) chicken or pork stock
2 cups (500 mL) canned diced tomatoes with their juice
½ cup (125 mL) cooked cannellini beans (drained and rinsed if canned)
5 fresh basil leaves, chopped
1 sprig fresh thyme, leaves only
Salt and pepper to taste
Extra virgin olive oil for garnish
Freshly grated Parmesan cheese for garnish

1. In a large cast iron pot over medium heat, sauté the onion in the oil, until the onion is softened.
2. Stir in the garlic. Sauté until the edges of the garlic start turning a light brown color and the mixture starts to feel tacky on the bottom of the pot when you stir it with a wooden spoon.
3. Add the kale and sausage. Sauté until the kale wilts, about 3 minutes.
4. Add the wine and cook until the boozy smell disappears, about 3 minutes.
5. Add the stock, tomatoes, beans, basil and thyme. Bring to a boil over high heat, then reduce the heat to medium-low.
6. Simmer, uncovered, until the sausage is cooked and the flavors have blended, about 20 minutes. Add salt and pepper to taste.
7. Take the pot to the table and serve family style, drizzling each hearty bowlful with olive oil and a sprinkling of Parmesan.

Pasta and Bean

Janis Kowall
Soup Sister

Makes about 4 servings

2 carrots, peeled and diced
2 stalks celery, diced
1 onion, diced
2 cloves garlic, minced or finely chopped
2 Tbsp (30 mL) vegetable oil
1 Tbsp (15 mL) finely chopped fresh basil leaves
½ tsp (2 mL) dried oregano leaves
4 cups (1 L) chicken or vegetable stock
1 can (19 oz/540 mL) kidney beans, drained and rinsed
2 cups (500 mL) canned crushed tomatoes
½ cup (125 mL) elbow macaroni
¼ cup (60 mL) finely chopped parsley
Salt and pepper to taste
¼ cup (60 mL) freshly grated Parmesan cheese

1. In a large pot over medium heat, sauté the carrots, celery, onion and garlic in the oil, until the onion is softened.
2. Stir in the basil and dried oregano.
3. Add the stock, beans and tomatoes. Bring to a boil over high heat, then reduce the heat to medium-low.
4. Simmer, uncovered, until the vegetables are tender, about 25 minutes.
5. Add the pasta, bring back to a simmer and cook, uncovered, until tender, about 15 minutes. Stir in the parsley and add salt and pepper to taste.
6. Ladle up a lovely chunky cup, and garnish with a stellar sprinkling of Parmesan.

When my kids were small and we were on tight schedules with hockey, art classes, tutors, carpools et cetera, this soup was a meal in itself and could be consumed on the move (without getting it all over the car!).
—*JANIS KOWALL*

Indian Red Lentil

Preena and Arvinda Chauhan
Owners, Arvinda's, spice blends and Indian cooking classes,
Toronto

vegetarian

gluten free

Makes about 4 servings

1 cup (250 mL) *masoor dal* (Indian split red lentils)
1 cup (250 mL) peeled and finely grated pumpkin
1 tsp (5 mL) salt (more to taste)
1 onion, diced
1 Tbsp (15 mL) ghee, clarified butter or unsalted butter
1 tsp (5 mL) minced or finely chopped garlic
1 tsp (5 mL) ground coriander
½ tsp (2 mL) ground cumin
¼ tsp (1 mL) chili powder
¼ tsp (1 mL) turmeric
¼ cup (60 mL) finely chopped cilantro
½ tsp (2 mL) garam masala

1. Wash the masoor dal in several changes of water until the water runs clear. Soak in a bowl of cold water for 10 minutes. Drain well.
2. Put the masoor dal, pumpkin, salt and 4 cups (1 L) water in a medium pot. Bring to a boil over high heat, then reduce the heat to medium-low.
3. Simmer, uncovered, until the lentils are tender, 10 to 15 minutes.
4. In a medium skillet over medium heat, sauté the onion in the ghee, until the onion is softened. Stir in the garlic, coriander, cumin, chili powder and turmeric.
5. Add the onion mixture to the masoor dal. Purée the soup until smooth.
6. Simmer, uncovered, for a further 10 to 15 minutes, adding extra water to thin out the soup to your desired consistency, if necessary. Add more salt to taste.
7. Serve a steamy bowlful garnished with cilantro and a sprinkling of garam masala.

Look for masoor dal and ghee in Indian grocery stores. While you're there, pick up some pappadums, too, and serve them alongside the soup for dipping. And, if you can, try to get hold of Arvinda's Garam Masala. Their spice mixes are truly like nothing else.

vegetarian

Winter Vegetable and Tofu Korma

Heidi Swanson
Cookbook Author and Blogger, 101cookbooks.com

 *gluten free*

Makes about 4 servings

1¾ tsp (9 mL) ground coriander
1½ tsp (7 mL) turmeric
1½ tsp (7 mL) red chili flakes
1½ tsp (7 mL) ground cumin
¼ tsp (1 mL) ground cardamom
¼ tsp (1 mL) ground cinnamon
2 onions, diced
2 Tbsp (30 mL) ghee or clarified butter
1 Tbsp (15 mL) grated fresh ginger
4 cloves garlic, minced or finely chopped
1½ lb (750 g) waxy potatoes, peeled and diced

12 oz (375 g) cauliflower, cut into tiny florets
⅔ cup (160 mL) toasted sliced almonds, divided
¾ tsp (4 mL) salt
12 oz (375 g) firm tofu, diced or cut into matchsticks
½ cup (125 mL) Greek yogurt
½ cup (125 mL) whipping cream (35% MF)
1 small bunch cilantro, finely chopped

An exotic array of spices and a market's worth of vegetables mean you won't miss the meat in this hearty, good-for-you, Indian-style soup. Feel free to use regular vegetable oil, such as sunflower oil, if you don't have ghee.

1. Combine the coriander, turmeric, red chili flakes, cumin, cardamom and cinnamon in a small bowl. Set aside.
2. In a large pot over medium heat, sauté the onions in the ghee, until the onions are softened.
3. Stir in the ginger, then the garlic. Stir in the spice mixture and cook until the spices are very fragrant, 1 to 2 minutes.
4. Stir in the potatoes, cauliflower, half of the almonds and the salt.
5. Add 3 cups (750 mL) water and stir gently. Bring to a boil over high heat, then reduce the heat to medium-low. Simmer, partially covered, until the potatoes are almost cooked, 15 minutes.
6. Stir in the tofu. Simmer until the potatoes are tender and the tofu is heated through, about 5 minutes.
7. Meanwhile, stir together the yogurt, cream and a pinch of salt in a bowl.
8. Reduce the heat to low and add the yogurt mixture all at once and bring the pot back just to the brink of a simmer. (Or serve the yogurt on the side, so people can make their bowl as rich as they like.) Add salt to the soup to taste.
9. Ladle up generous servings topped with cilantro and almonds.

Beef and Barley

Becky Hapton
Soup Sister

Makes about 6 servings

1 lb (500 g) beef short ribs
2 Tbsp (30 mL) kosher salt or sea salt
6 stalks celery, diced
3 onions, diced
2 parsnips, peeled and diced
20 button mushrooms, quartered
1¼ cups (310 mL) pot barley
1 can (19 oz/540 mL) diced tomatoes
3 cloves garlic, minced or finely chopped
Salt and pepper to taste
3 sprigs fresh dill, finely chopped

Sometimes the classic combos are the best, and isn't beef and barley a marriage just made in heaven? This is definitely a soup that tastes even better the next day. Just discard any fat that's risen to and solidified on the top.

1. Place the short ribs in a large pot and add 6 cups (1.5 L) water and the salt.
2. Bring to a boil over high heat. Skim off the foam that rises to the surface.
3. Pile in the celery, onions, parsnips, mushrooms, barley, tomatoes and garlic. Bring back to a simmer, then reduce the heat to medium-low.
4. Pop a lid on the pot and simmer until the ribs are tender, about 4 hours. Add salt and pepper to taste.
5. Ladle up a chunky bowlful of meaty, melty ribs with vegetables, and garnish with a sprinkling of dill.

Mom's Chicken

Sandy Mowat
Soup Sister

Makes about 6 servings

6 cups (1.5 L) chicken stock
3 skinless, boneless chicken breasts, diced
3 carrots, peeled and diced
3 stalks celery, diced
2 zucchini, diced
⅓ cup (80 mL) long-grain white rice
¼ cup (60 mL) unsalted butter
¼ cup (60 mL) all-purpose flour
2 cups (500 mL) milk
Salt and pepper to taste
½ cup (125 mL) sliced green onions
¼ cup (60 mL) finely chopped parsley

1. Pour the stock into a large pot. Pile in the chicken, carrots, celery, zucchini and rice.
2. Bring to a boil over high heat, then reduce the heat to medium-low.
3. Simmer, uncovered, until the rice is tender and the chicken is cooked through, about 25 minutes.
4. Melt the butter in a small saucepan over medium-high heat. Sprinkle in the flour, stirring until the mixture forms a cohesive clump. Slowly whisk in the milk until smooth.
5. Whisk a couple of ladles of soup into the sauce. Stirring constantly, bring the sauce to a boil, then boil and stir for 2 minutes to activate the thickening power of the flour.
6. Now pour the creamy mixture into the large pot and whisk to incorporate it into the soup. As soon as it comes to a boil, reduce the heat to low. Add salt and pepper to taste.
7. Ladle up a hot and creamy bowl of fond family memories in the making, garnish with a motherly sprinkling of green onions and parsley.

Everyone knows that when you're sick the secret to bringing you back to health is chicken soup. And the better the soup, the sooner you'll be up and running around!

French Onion

Christine Straub
Soup Sister

Makes 6 servings

3 Tbsp (45 mL) unsalted butter
4 onions, peeled and diced
8 cups (2 L) beef stock
6 slices French bread, cut 1 inch (2.5 cm) thick
½ cup (125 mL) shredded Gruyère cheese
¼ cup (60 mL) freshly grated Parmesan cheese
Salt and pepper to taste

1. Melt the butter in a large pot over medium heat. Sauté the onions until well browned, about 40 minutes.
2. Add the stock. Bring to a boil over high heat, then reduce the heat to medium-low.
3. Simmer, uncovered, until the onions are very tender, about 30 minutes.
4. While the soup simmers, preheat the oven to 425°F (220°C). Sprinkle the bread slices with lots of Gruyère, then top with Parmesan. Arrange the slices on a baking sheet and bake until they're nice and golden and bubbly on top, about 5 minutes.
5. Add salt and pepper to taste to the soup.
6. Ladle up piping hot bowl of onion soup and top with a bubbly, cheesy round of toast. Give the bread a minute or two to soak up the action before eating.

Usually the onions for French onion soup are sliced into thin strips, but that causes strings of cooked onion to hang over the edge of the spoon where they can burn your chin! So we prefer to dice the onions instead.

vegetarian

Dill Pickle

Kathleen Houston
Soup Sister

Makes about 4 servings

1 onion, sliced
2 Tbsp (30 mL) unsalted butter
4 cups (1 L) chicken or vegetable stock
4 large potatoes, peeled and diced
4 large garlic dill pickles, chopped (about 3 cups/750 mL)
⅔ cup (160 mL) liquid from pickle jar, or water
1 cup (250 mL) sour cream
2 Tbsp (30 mL) all-purpose flour
Salt and pepper to taste
Sugar to taste (optional)
Chopped fresh dill for garnish

1. In a large pot over medium heat, sauté the onion in the butter, until the onion is softened.
2. Add the stock, potatoes, pickles and pickle liquid. Bring to a boil over high heat, then reduce heat to low.
3. Simmer, uncovered, until the potatoes are tender, about 20 minutes.
4. In a bowl, blend together the sour cream and flour until smooth. Whisk a little of the hot soup into the sour cream mixture.
5. Add the sour cream to the hot soup. Bring to a boil over high heat, whisking constantly, then reduce the heat to medium-low. Simmer, uncovered, until slightly thickened, about 3 minutes.
6. Purée the soup until smooth or leave it chunky. Add salt and pepper to taste, and sugar, if you like.
7. Serve a creamy bowlful, garnished with chopped fresh dill.

Before refrigeration, pickling was a common way of preserving fruits, vegetables, meats and eggs in Poland and other parts of Eastern Europe. Pickled baby cucumbers in hot broth was the winter counterpart to the summer offering of cold cucumber soup. In my family, we made dill pickle soup with a ketchup base. This more widely known variation uses sour cream.

—KATHLEEN HOUSTON

Budapest Night Owl

Kalayra Angelyys
Soup Sister

Makes about 8 servings

1 bone-in ham shank, about
  2 lb (1 kg)
8 slices bacon, chopped
1 onion, diced
2 Tbsp (30 mL) unsalted butter
¼ cup (60 mL) all-purpose flour
3 Tbsp (45 mL) sweet Hungarian
  paprika, divided
2 Tbsp (30 mL) sweet smoked
  Spanish paprika, divided

2 jars (28 oz/796 mL each)
  sauerkraut
½ lb (250 g) dry-cured hot chorizo,
  diced
1 cup (250 mL) sour cream
Salt and pepper to taste
Sweet Hungarian paprika for garnish

1. The day before you want to eat the soup, put the ham shank in a large pot and add 3 quarts (3 L) water.
2. Bring to a boil over high heat, skimming away any scum that rises to the surface. Reduce the heat to medium-low. Simmer, uncovered, for 2 hours.
3. Remove the shank, reserving the stock. Let cool, then remove the meat from the bone. Dice the meat, discarding the bone. Cover and refrigerate the meat and stock separately overnight.
4. The next day, in a large pot over medium heat, sauté the bacon and onion in the butter, until the onion is softened. Sprinkle in the flour and half the Hungarian and Spanish paprikas.
5. Add the sauerkraut, with its brine, and the stock to the pot. Bring to a boil over high heat. Boil for 1 minute to activate the thickening power of the flour, then reduce the heat to medium-low.
6. Add the diced ham and chorizo to the pot. Simmer, uncovered, for 2 hours to blend the flavors.
7. Just before serving, stir together the sour cream and the remaining paprikas in a small bowl. Stir the sour cream into the soup and add salt and pepper to taste.
8. Ladle up a chunky bowlful of stewy goodness, and top with a cheeky dash of paprika for added sassiness.

The Hungarians are famous for their paprika. But so, too, are the Spanish. The big difference between the two spices is that Spanish paprika is smoked, while Hungarian paprika is not.

My Big, Fat Italian Wedding

Jennifer Low
Cookbook Author

Makes about 6 servings

Mini Meatballs

1½ lb (750 g) meatloaf mix (a mixture of ground beef, pork and veal)
⅓ cup (80 mL) freshly grated Parmesan or Romano cheese
⅓ cup (80 mL) milk
1 Tbsp (15 mL) dried parsley leaves
1 tsp (5 mL) dried oregano leaves
1 tsp (5 mL) minced or finely chopped garlic
1 tsp (5 mL) salt
¼ tsp (1 mL) black pepper
Pinch of grated nutmeg

Soup

8 cups (2 L) chicken stock
2 carrots, peeled and thinly sliced
2 stalks celery with leaves, diced
1 onion, diced
4 cloves garlic, roughly crushed
½ tsp (2 mL) dried oregano leaves
1 bay leaf
8 to 10 skinless, bone-in chicken drumsticks (about 2 lb/1 kg)
1 cup (250 mL) orzo or other small pasta
2 handfuls chopped escarole or spinach
⅓ cup (80 mL) freshly grated Parmesan or Romano cheese
1 Tbsp (15 mL) basil pesto
Freshly grated Parmesan or Romano cheese for garnish (optional)

I think when it comes to making homemade soups, if it's not chock-full of ingredients, why bother? This recipe takes chicken soup to a whole other level of heartiness. It's sublimely chickeny (in my house that's a real word!), even if you don't start with homemade stock.

—*Jennifer Low*

1. For the mini meatballs, mix together all the ingredients in a large bowl. Pinch off pieces the size of cranberries (they do not need to be round). Set aside on a large plate.

2. For the soup, combine the stock, carrots, celery, onion, garlic, oregano, bay leaf and 4 cups (1 L) water in a large pot. Bring to a boil over high heat, then reduce the heat to medium-low.

3. Drop the mini meatballs into the simmering soup in batches. Add the chicken drumsticks. Simmer, covered, until the chicken meat begins to pull away from the bones, about 20 minutes.

4. Stir in the orzo and escarole. Simmer, partially covered and stirring occasionally, until the orzo is tender, about 20 minutes.

5. Remove the pot from the heat. Remove the bay leaf. Stir in the Parmesan cheese and basil pesto.

6. Ladle up steamy servings scattered with additional grated cheese, if liked.

If you prefer to serve the soup without the chicken bones, remove the drumsticks with a slotted spoon before you add the orzo and escarole. Pull off the meat in rough shreds. Chop the meat and return it to the soup. Add the orzo and escarole, and continue with the recipe.

Hungarian Beef Goulash

Anna Olson
Cookbook Author and Host of *Fresh with Anna Olson*

Makes about 4 servings

3 slices bacon, diced
1½ lb (750 g) boneless blade roast, cut into ½-inch (1 cm) pieces
2 onions, diced
1 large carrot, peeled and diced
1 parsnip, peeled and diced
1 stalk celery, diced
2 Tbsp (30 mL) sweet Hungarian paprika
2 cloves garlic, minced or finely chopped
2 tsp (10 mL) finely chopped fresh thyme
1 tsp (5 mL) caraway seeds (optional)
2 bay leaves
4 cups (1 L) beef stock (use low-sodium if store-bought)
1 can (28 oz/796 mL) diced tomatoes
Salt and pepper to taste
Csipetke (see next page)
Sour cream for garnish

1. Heat a large pot over medium heat. Sauté the bacon until crisp. Remove the bacon with a slotted spoon and drain on a paper-towel-lined plate. Pour off all but 2 Tbsp (30 mL) of the bacon fat from the pot.
2. Increase the heat to high. Brown the beef, in batches. Transfer the browned beef to a bowl.
3. Sauté the onions, carrot, parsnip and celery in the same pot over medium heat until the onions are softened.
4. Stir in the paprika, garlic, thyme, caraway seeds (if using) and bay leaves. Cook, stirring, for 1 minute.
5. Return the beef to the pot, along with the stock and tomatoes. Bring to a boil over high heat, then reduce the heat to medium-low.

continued next page

The chills from a cold wintry day are completely banished when you smell the hearty aromas of a simmering goulash. I think of it as a cross between a soup and a stew. The little homemade noodles (which are more like tender dumplings) are the added touch that make goulash that much more heartwarming.
—ANNA OLSON

6. Simmer, covered, until the beef is tender, about 90 minutes. Remove the bay leaves. Add salt and pepper to taste.
7. Prepare the *csipetke* (see below) and add to the goulash.
8. Serve the goulash in wide bowls topped with dollops of sour cream and a scattering of crispy bacon.

Csipetke

Csipetke are Hungarian pinched noodles that are perfect with the goulash.

1. Whisk 1 **egg** lightly, then stir in ½ cup (125 mL) **all-purpose flour** and a pinch of **salt** until well combined. The dough should be dense but a little stretchy and you should be able to pick it up and handle it with your hands. If it's too dense, add a little water.
2. Using floured hands, pinch off little pea-size pieces of the dough and drop into the simmering goulash. Simmer for 5 minutes before serving.

Mexican Pozole

Jennifer Bain
Food Editor, *Toronto Star*

Makes about 6 servings

6 regular or 4 extra-large chicken
bouillon cubes
1 small onion, quartered
8 cloves garlic
1 Tbsp (15 mL) coriander seeds
2½ lb (1.25 kg) piece bone-in pork
butt, cut in half and fat trimmed
slightly
5 bay leaves
1 can (29 oz/822 g) white hominy,
drained and rinsed
Dried oregano leaves
Pequin chili powder or other pure
chili powder (optional)

Toppings (optional)
Shredded iceberg lettuce (from
1 small head)
Sliced avocado
Fresh cilantro
Sliced radishes
Minced white onion
Lime quarters

1. Combine the bouillon cubes, onion, garlic, coriander seeds and 1 cup (250 mL) water in a countertop blender. Blend for 1 minute. Press the mixture through a fine-mesh sieve, discarding the solids. Set the bouillon liquid aside.
2. Put the pork and bay leaves in a large pot. Add 8 cups (2 L) water. Bring to a boil over high heat, then reduce the heat to medium. Simmer, covered, for 30 minutes.
3. Add the reserved bouillon liquid. Simmer, covered, until the pork pulls apart with two forks, 60 to 90 minutes.
4. Remove the pork to a cutting board and let cool slightly. Discard the fat and bones. Shred the meat by hand or with two forks.
5. Remove the bay leaves from the pot. Add the hominy. Cook over high heat, stirring occasionally, for about 5 minutes or until heated through.
6. Add the shredded pork. Cook for 1 to 2 minutes or until heated through.
7. Arrange the toppings on a serving plate. Ladle up a steaming, hearty bowlful of pozole. Garnish with a sprinkling of oregano and chili powder (if using).

One of the joys of urban life is going out for a soulful bowl of pozole at a Mexican restaurant. Shredded meat (usually pork or chicken) and hominy (derived from corn) form the substantial backdrop, and then, with a generous plate of garnishes, you can personalize your bowl with a riot of flavors. I learned this version years ago from the owner of El Camino restaurant in Toronto.
—*JENNIFER BAIN*

Big Lou's Meat Hook Chili

Karl Gregg
Chef/Owner, 2 Chefs and a Table, and Co-owner, Big Lou's
  Butcher Shop, Vancouver

Makes about 4 servings

  2 Tbsp (30 mL) vegetable oil
  1 lb (500 g) ground beef
  2 carrots, peeled and grated
  2 stalks celery, diced
  1 onion, diced
  1 Tbsp (15 mL) dried oregano leaves
  1 Tbsp (15 mL) adobo sauce (see sidebar)
  2 tsp (10 mL) chili powder
  1 tsp (5 mL) ground cumin
  1 can (19 oz/540 mL) black beans, drained and rinsed
  1 can (19 oz/540 mL) red kidney beans, drained and rinsed
  1 can (19 oz/540 mL) diced tomatoes
Salt and pepper to taste

Canned chipotle chilies in adobo sauce are spicy-hot smoked jalapeños. Use just the sauce for this recipe. The rest of the can may be frozen to use in other recipes.

1. Heat a large pot over medium-high heat. Add the oil. When the oil is hot, sauté the ground beef, carrots, celery and onion until the beef is browned and the onion is softened.
2. Stir in the oregano, adobo sauce, chili powder and cumin.
3. Add the black beans, kidney beans and tomatoes. Bring to a boil over high heat, then reduce the heat to medium-low.
4. Simmer, uncovered, until the beef is cooked, about 30 minutes, adding a little water if the chili seems to be too thick. Add salt and pepper to taste.
5. Ladle up a piping hot bowl of chili and enjoy with something frothy gold and frosty cold.

Hungarian Cabbage Soup

Sylvia Dioszegi
Soup Sister

Makes about 6 servings

1 medium cabbage, cored and chopped
3 carrots, peeled and thinly sliced
2 parsnips, peeled and thinly sliced
2 stalks celery, diced
1 onion, diced
1 green pepper, seeded and diced
1 Tbsp (15 mL) all-purpose flour
1½ tsp (7 mL) sweet Hungarian paprika (optional)
Salt and pepper to taste

1. Put the cabbage, carrots, parsnips, celery, onion and green pepper in a large pot. Add about 1 inch (2.5 cm) of water (just enough to steam the vegetables). Bring to a boil over medium-high heat. Cover with a tight-fitting lid and steam until the vegetables are half-cooked.
2. In a small bowl, mix the flour with 2 Tbsp (30 mL) water until smooth.
3. Add more water to the pot until the vegetables are submerged. Bring to a boil over high heat, then reduce the heat to medium-low.
4. Add the flour mixture and paprika (if using) to the pot. Simmer, uncovered, until the vegetables are tender and the soup has thickened, 20 to 30 minutes. Add salt and pepper to taste.
5. Serve up a hearty vegetable-rich portion and feel good about yourself.

Let's be honest here. The recipe says the paprika is optional. But if you leave it out you'll also need to drop *Hungarian* from the name and then it will just be called Cabbage Soup. Which would you rather have? We thought so!

The SOUPS of SPRING

The long, cold winter is done and, ever so slowly, the world is becoming greener. Birds and butterflies (and some people, too!) are on their way home from spending the cooler months down south. Spring has sprung, and the great outdoors is opening up for business.

Now's a great time do a little spring cleaning in the kitchen and defrost any frozen stock you have left from the winter months. Use it to simmer up a lovely bowlful from our lineup of lighter, springtime soups. We have some starring seafood, others rich with vegetables and herbs. Either way, they'll lighten your mood and chase away the last of winter's chill.

vegetarian

gluten free

Sweet Garlic and Sunchoke

Michael Allemeier
Chef and Culinary Instructor at SAIT (Southern Alberta Institute of
Technology), Calgary

Makes about 6 servings

2 lb (1 kg) Jerusalem artichokes, scrubbed (see sidebar)
⅓ cup (80 mL) canola oil
2 large onions, diced
2 leeks, white and pale green parts only, washed and sliced
15 whole cloves garlic
2 Tbsp (30 mL) unsalted butter
8 cups (2 L) chicken or vegetable stock (approx.)
Salt to taste
Sunchoke chips for garnish (see below)

1. Preheat the oven to 400°F (200°C). Toss the artichokes in the oil and
   spread out in a single layer in a large roasting pan. Roast until the
   artichokes are golden and tender, about 30 minutes.
2. In a large pot over medium heat, sauté the onions, leeks and garlic in
   the butter, until the onions are softened. Add the artichokes.
3. Add in enough stock to cover the artichokes. Bring to a boil over high
   heat, then reduce the heat to medium-low. Simmer, uncovered, until
   the garlic is tender, about 30 minutes.
4. Purée the soup until smooth. Reheat over medium heat and add salt
   to taste.
5. Serve a steamy, creamy bowl with some crunchy fried sunchoke chips.

Sunchoke Chips

Scrub 2 or 3 **Jerusalem artichokes** and cut them into very thin slices (use a
mandoline slicer if you have one). Pat the slices dry. Heat a little **canola oil**
in a skillet over medium-high heat. Fry the artichoke slices until crisp and
golden brown. Drain on a paper-towel-lined plate and sprinkle liberally
with **salt**.

Sunchoke is another name for the Jerusalem artichoke. This tuber is actually a member of the sunflower family and not an artichoke at all. It has an earthy flavor, reminiscent of sunflower seeds.
—MICHAEL ALLEMEIER

Celeriac and Apple with Maple Cream

Wanda Chau
Blogger, bahbakedathome.com

Makes about 4 servings

4 slices bacon, diced
1 onion, diced
3 Tbsp (45 mL) unsalted butter
1 celeriac, peeled and diced
1 potato, peeled and diced
½ cup (125 mL) dry vermouth

4 cups (1 L) chicken stock
3 apples, peeled, cored and
  diced
Maple cream (see below)
Juice of 1 lemon
Salt and pepper to taste

1. Heat a large pot over medium heat. Sauté the bacon until crispy. Remove the bacon with a slotted spoon and drain on a paper-towel-lined plate to use as a garnish later.
2. Add the onion and butter to the bacon fat remaining in the pot. Sauté until the onion is softened. Stir in the celeriac and potato.
3. Add the dry vermouth and boil until it has reduced by half.
4. Add the stock and apples. Bring to a boil over high heat, then reduce the heat to medium-low.
5. Simmer, uncovered, until the potato and celeriac are tender, about 20 minutes.
6. While the soup simmers, make the maple cream (see below).
7. Purée the soup until smooth. If the soup is too thick, thin it down with a little hot water until it is the desired consistency. Reheat the soup and add the lemon juice, and the salt and pepper to taste.
8. Ladle up a sweet and steamy bowl, and garnish with a grandiose flourish of maple cream and some crispy bacon.

Maple Cream
1 cup (250 mL) sour cream
⅓ cup (80 mL) maple syrup
1 Tbsp (15 mL) finely chopped fresh thyme

In a small bowl, stir together all of the ingredients. Leave it to infuse while the soup boils. The maple cream is also great for dipping apple slices.

Matzoh Ball

Marcy Goldman
Pastry Chef and Cookbook Author

Makes about 6 servings

Matzoh balls (see right)
1 chicken, preferably kosher (4 to 5 lb/1.8 to 2.2 kg)
Extra chicken legs and wings (optional)
2 large stalks celery with a few leaves, left whole
2 large carrots, peeled and cut into 3-inch (8 cm) chunks
2 parsnips, peeled and cut into 3-inch (8 cm) chunks
1 onion, cut in half
½ cup (125 mL) finely chopped parsley, divided
½ cup (125 mL) roughly chopped fresh dill
1 Tbsp (15 mL) whole black peppercorns
1 cup (250 mL) diced celery
1 cup (250 mL) diced carrots
2 Tbsp (30 mL) finely chopped fresh dill
Salt and pepper to taste

The diced fresh vegetables added to this soup toward the end of cooking time are for eye and taste appeal. The celery stalks, carrot and parsnip chunks, onion and chicken carcass added at the beginning are what give the soup its flavor. They did their duty and can be discarded when you strain the soup.

1. Prepare the matzoh balls.
2. Rinse the chicken well and place it in a large stockpot. Add the extra wings and legs (if using) and enough cold water to the pot to just cover the top of the chicken. Bring to a boil over high heat, skimming off any foam that forms.
3. Add the whole celery stalks, carrot and parsnip chunks, onion, all but 2 Tbsp (30 mL) of the parsley, roughly chopped dill and black peppercorns. Reduce the heat to medium.
4. Cover partially and simmer for about 2 hours. When the soup is done, it should taste brothy, not watery. Let cool slightly.
5. Strain the soup, discarding the chicken skin and bones, vegetables and flavorings. Save the choice pieces of chicken for a chicken salad, or to add back, in smaller pieces, to the soup.
6. If you're not serving the soup right away, refrigerate it overnight and skim off the fat from the surface the next day.

7. Pour the soup into a clean pot and add the diced celery and carrots, remaining parsley, finely chopped dill and salt and pepper to taste.

8. Bring back to a simmer and cook, uncovered, until the diced vegetables are just tender.

9. Ladle the matzoh balls carefully into the soup. Reheat gently.

10. Ladle the lovely chickeny broth into bowls, adding 1 or 2 matzoh balls per bowl.

Matzoh Balls

1 cup (250 mL) matzoh meal
2½ tsp (12 mL) salt, divided
Pinch of black pepper
4 eggs, lightly beaten
⅓ cup (80 mL) olive oil
2 Tbsp (30 mL) water

1. Stir together the matzoh meal, ½ tsp (2 mL) of the salt and a pinch of pepper.

2. In a small bowl, whisk together the eggs, oil and water.

3. Add the egg mixture to the matzoh meal. Blend well and let stand (at room temperature or in the refrigerator) for 20 minutes or until the mixture is firm enough that you can handle it and form it into balls.

4. Fill a Dutch oven or large pot three-quarters full with water and add the remaining salt. Bring to a rolling boil.

5. With wet or oiled hands (or wear latex gloves, which are helpful for messy kitchen jobs like this), form spoonfuls of matzoh mixture into 3-inch (8 cm) balls.

6. Gently drop the balls into the boiling water. Reduce the heat to low, cover the pot and simmer the matzoh balls for 30 minutes or until they have expanded and are set.

7. With a slotted spoon, gently remove the matzoh balls from the water and drain them. Set aside in a single layer on a large plate.

Matzoh meal is ground matzoh, the thin unleavened bread eaten at Passover. You can also use it for breading chicken or fish before frying. Look for matzoh meal in larger supermarkets or Jewish grocery stores. If you prefer, you can add freshly cooked egg noodles to the soup instead of matzoh balls.

Silky Jerusalem Artichoke

Lucy Waverman
Cookbook Author and Columnist

Makes about 4 servings

1½ cups (375 mL) diced onion
1 tsp (5 mL) chopped garlic
2 Tbsp (30 mL) unsalted butter
4 cups (1 L) peeled and diced Jerusalem artichokes
4 cups (1 L) chicken or vegetable stock
⅓ cup (80 mL) whipping cream (35% MF)
Pinch of cayenne
Salt and pepper to taste
2 Tbsp (30 mL) chopped fresh chives
Shavings of Parmesan cheese for garnish
Additional whipping cream for garnish

Jerusalem artichokes aren't from Jerusalem. Nor are they artichokes, but they do provide a similar flavor to this sophisticated, creamy soup. Peel the knobby artichokes with a small paring knife.

1. In a large pot over medium heat, sauté the onion and garlic in the butter, until the onion is softened.
2. Stir in the artichokes. Sauté for 1 minute.
3. Add the stock. Bring to a boil over high heat, then reduce the heat to medium-low.
4. Simmer, covered, until the artichokes are tender, about 15 minutes.
5. Purée the soup until smooth. Add the cream. Reheat over medium heat and add the pinch of cayenne and salt and pepper to taste.
6. Serve up a creamy, earthy bowlful, and add zip with a sprinkling of chives, some Parmesan shavings and a swirl of cream.

Comforting Egg Drop and Parmesan

Linda Haynes and Devin Connell
Cookbook Authors

Makes about 4 servings

4 cups (1 L) chicken or vegetable stock
½ tsp (2 mL) cornstarch
1 egg
1 Tbsp (15 mL) finely chopped parsley
1 Tbsp (15 mL) finely chopped fresh chives
1 tsp (5 mL) lemon zest
½ tsp (2 mL) finely chopped fresh thyme
¼ tsp (1 mL) black pepper
½ cup (125 mL) freshly grated Parmesan cheese

1. In a large pot, bring the stock to a boil over high heat.
2. Meanwhile, stir together the cornstarch and 1 tsp (5 mL) water in a small pitcher or measuring cup.
3. Add the egg to the cornstarch mixture and beat with a fork until well combined.
4. Remove the pot from the heat. Without stirring the stock, slowly drizzle very thin streams of the egg mixture into the pot in a circular motion. Let the soup sit for 1 minute.
5. Return the pot to medium-high heat and bring the soup to a simmer. Immediately remove the pot from the heat.
6. Stir in the parsley, chives, lemon zest, thyme and pepper. Use the bottom of a ladle to break up any large pieces of egg.
7. Ladle up a comforting bowlful and scatter with Parmesan cheese.

This recipe is excerpted from Two Dishes *by Linda Haynes and Devin Connell (McClelland and Stewart, 2009).*

This soup serves me very well when I'm feeling under the weather. It's easy on the tummy and nourishing. Adding the cornstarch to the raw egg makes the egg incredibly silky and light by stabilizing the liquid proteins when they are heated, so there's no shrinkage and no rubbery texture. I eat this with lots of crusty bread. My Mom, Linda Haynes, sometimes adds a cooked and shredded chicken breast.
—DEVIN CONNELL

Mushroom with Thyme Croutons

Andrew Richardson
Executive Chef/Co-owner, Blink Restaurant and Bar, Calgary

Makes about 8 servings

2 Tbsp (30 mL) unsalted butter
2 lb (1 kg) button mushrooms, sliced
1 onion, diced
1 leek, white and pale green parts only, washed and sliced
Thyme croutons (see below)
6 cups (1.5 L) chicken or vegetable stock
6 cups (1.5 L) whipping cream (35% MF)
1 potato, peeled and diced
Salt and pepper to taste

This is a classic chef's recipe. How can you tell? It tastes amazing, and there's a lot (and we mean *a lot*) of cream in it. But indulge; it's worth it.

1. Melt the butter in a large pot over medium heat. Add the mushrooms, onion and leek. Cook, covered, until the mushrooms and onion are softened.
2. While the vegetables soften, prepare the thyme croutons (see below).
3. Add the stock, cream and potato to the pot. Bring to a boil over high heat, then reduce the heat to medium-low.
4. Simmer, uncovered, until the potato is tender, about 15 minutes.
5. Purée the soup until smooth. Reheat over medium heat and add salt and pepper to taste.
6. Ladle up a steamy, creamy bowl and scatter with crispy, herby croutons.

Thyme Croutons

1. Drizzle 2 cups (500 mL) **cubed bread** (or sliced baguette) with ¼ cup (60 mL) **olive oil**, tossing to coat the bread as you pour in the oil. Add 1 Tbsp (15 mL) finely chopped **fresh thyme**, and sprinkle generously with **salt and pepper**. Toss again.
2. Spread out the bread cubes in a single layer on a rimmed baking sheet. Bake in a 350°F (180°C) oven until crisp and golden, about 15 minutes.

Manhattan Clam Chowder

Shawn Greenwood
Executive Chef, Taste, Calgary

Makes about 6 servings

4 slices bacon, chopped
4 stalks celery, diced
2 sweet red peppers, seeded and diced
1 onion, diced
1 Tbsp (15 mL) Old Bay Seasoning
3 Tbsp (45 mL) unsalted butter
3 Tbsp (45 mL) all-purpose flour
4 cups (1 L) chicken stock
1 cup (250 mL) clam juice
1 can (28 oz/796 mL) diced tomatoes
2 russet potatoes, peeled and diced
1½ lb (750 g) clam meat (see sidebar)
Salt and pepper to taste
Freshly cracked black pepper for garnish

Frozen clam meat can be bought in large bags at fish stores or specialty markets. Alternatively, you can use canned clam meat. Drain off the juices and rinse the clams lightly or your soup will be super salty.

1. Heat a large pot over medium heat. Sauté the bacon until browned but not crispy.
2. Add the celery, red peppers, onion and Old Bay Seasoning. Sauté until the onion is softened.
3. Add the butter, stirring until it melts and the vegetables are glossy.
4. Sprinkle the flour evenly over the vegetables. Stir well to combine.
5. Gradually stir in the stock and clam juice. Bring to a boil over high heat, stirring all the time. Boil and stir for 2 minutes until slightly thickened.
6. Add the tomatoes and potatoes and reduce the heat to low.
7. Simmer, uncovered, until the potatoes are tender, about 25 minutes.
8. Add the clam meat. Bring the soup back to a simmer and add salt and pepper to taste.
9. Ladle up a piping vessel of chowder, topped with fresh cracked pepper.

Thai Chicken and Coconut Milk

Rina Grunwald
Soup Sister

Makes about 4 servings

2 skinless, boneless chicken breasts, diced
Zest and juice of 1 lime
1 stalk lemongrass (see sidebar)
2 cans (14 oz/398 mL each) unsweetened coconut milk
1 Tbsp (15 mL) grated galangal or fresh ginger (see sidebar)
1 bird's eye chili, split in half lengthwise
Salt to taste
½ bunch cilantro, roughly chopped

1. In a large bowl, toss the chicken with the zest and juice of lime. Set aside.
2. Trim off a thin slice from the root end of the lemongrass and discard. Cut off the dry, upper half of the stalk and discard. With the back of a chef's knife, bash the tender part of the stalk a few times to release its aroma, then cut it into 2-inch (5 cm) lengths.
3. Combine the lemongrass, coconut milk, galangal and chili in a large pot. Bring to a gentle simmer over medium heat. Simmer, uncovered, to blend the flavors, about 15 minutes.
4. Add the chicken and bring back to a simmer. Cook until the chicken is tender and cooked through, 15 to 20 minutes.
5. Remove the lemongrass and chili (they add amazing flavor but aren't the most pleasant things to have in your mouth). Add salt to taste.
6. Ladle up a hot chunky vessel, and garnish with a grandiose scattering of cilantro.

Lemongrass is a very tough and woody grass with loads of bright citrus aroma. It's best to use the more tender, bottom end of the stalk.

Galangal, like ginger, is the edible bulbous root or rhizome of a plant. Galangal tastes similar to ginger but packs a pleasing peppery flavor. If you can't find frozen galangal in a specialty or Asian grocery store, you can use ginger.

This quick and easy recipe is a favorite of my kids and reminds them of our trip to Bali, a part of the world where the people are warm and loving and share everything, including their soup recipes.
—RINA GRUNWALD

vegetarian

Carrot, Leek and Rice

Elizabeth Baird
Food Writer and Cookbook Author

Makes about 4 servings

6 carrots, peeled and diced
2 leeks, white and pale green parts only, washed and sliced
2 cloves garlic, minced or finely chopped
1 Tbsp (15 mL) unsalted butter
½ tsp (2 mL) dried thyme leaves
¼ tsp (1 mL) dried oregano leaves
1 bay leaf
4 cups (1 L) chicken or vegetable stock
¼ cup (60 mL) long-grain white rice
1 cup (250 mL) frozen peas
Juice of 1 lemon
Salt and pepper to taste
Cheese toasts for garnish (see below)

This is one of those soul-satisfying soups that's perfect when you are sick or need to feed someone who has one of those pesky head colds that seem to linger into spring.

1. In a large pot over medium heat, sauté the carrots, leeks and garlic in the butter, until the leeks are softened.
2. Stir in the thyme, oregano and bay leaf. Add the stock and rice. Bring to a boil over high heat, then reduce the heat to medium-low.
3. Simmer, uncovered, until the rice is tender, about 15 minutes (about 30 minutes for brown rice). At the last minute, add the peas, just to heat through.
4. Remove the bay leaf. Add the lemon juice, and salt and pepper to taste.
5. Ladle up a lovely, bubbly bowl, and garnish with cheese toasts.

Cheese Toasts
Preheat the oven to 400°F (200°C). Trim the crusts from 4 large slices of **bread**. Drizzle with **olive oil** and top with shredded **white cheddar cheese**. Place on a baking sheet, and bake in the oven until the cheese has melted and the bread is nice and crispy, about 8 minutes. Cut each slice into bite-size squares.

Rosemary, Garlic and Chickpea

Karen Miller
Soup Sister

Makes about 4 servings

1 onion, diced
¼ cup (60 mL) olive oil
¼ cup (60 mL) fresh rosemary leaves, finely chopped
4 cloves garlic, minced or finely chopped
2 cans (19 oz/540 mL each) chickpeas, drained and rinsed
1 Tbsp (15 mL) tomato paste
4 cups (1 L) chicken or vegetable stock
Salt and pepper to taste
Freshly grated Parmesan cheese for garnish

1. In a large pot over medium heat, sauté the onion in the oil, until the onion is softened.
2. Stir in the rosemary and garlic.
3. Stir in the chickpeas and tomato paste. Sauté for 5 minutes until glossy.
4. Add the stock. Bring to a boil over high heat, then reduce the heat to medium-low.
5. Simmer, uncovered, until the soup has thickened and the flavors have blended, about 30 minutes. Add salt and pepper to taste.
6. Ladle up a chunky cup, and garnish with some punchy Parmesan.

Easy and Delish Mushroom

Cindy Groner
Soup Sister

Makes about 4 servings

3 Tbsp (45 mL) unsalted butter, divided
1 Tbsp (15 mL) all-purpose flour
1 cup (250 mL) milk
½ lb (250 g) button mushrooms, sliced
1 onion, diced
1 clove garlic, minced or finely chopped
2 cups (500 mL) chicken or vegetable stock
½ cup (125 mL) whipping cream (35% MF)
1 tsp (5 mL) Dijon mustard
1 tsp (5 mL) Worcestershire sauce
Pinch of grated nutmeg
Salt and pepper to taste
¼ cup (60 mL) finely chopped parsley

1. Start by making a béchamel sauce. Melt 1 Tbsp (15 mL) of the butter in a small saucepan over medium heat. Stir in the flour until it forms lumps. Whisking constantly, slowly add the milk. Continue whisking until you have a thick, smooth paste. Set aside.
2. In a large pot over medium heat, sauté the mushrooms, onion and garlic in the remaining butter, until the mushrooms and onion are softened.
3. Stir in the béchamel sauce until well combined.
4. Gradually whisk in the stock until smooth. Bring to a boil over high heat, then reduce the heat to medium-low.
5. Simmer, stirring often, until thickened and smooth, about 10 minutes.
6. Stir in the cream, mustard, Worcestershire sauce and nutmeg. Reheat over medium heat and add salt and pepper to taste.
7. Ladle up a steamy bowl, and garnish with a cheeky smattering of parsley.

Béchamel sauce, made from butter, flour and milk, is used as the base of many cream sauces and helps to thicken this soup.

The Real Deal Bouillabaisse

Terry Groner
Soup Sister

Makes about 4 servings

2 carrots, peeled and diced
2 stalks celery, diced
1 onion, diced
1 leek, white and pale green parts only, washed and sliced
5 Tbsp (75 mL) olive oil
3 cloves garlic, minced or finely chopped
1 tsp (5 mL) red chili flakes
2 bay leaves
Pinch of saffron threads
4 tomatoes, seeded and diced
2 potatoes, peeled and diced
½ cup (125 mL) white wine
2 Tbsp (30 mL) tomato paste
8 cups (2 L) fish stock
Rouille (see right)
1 lb (500 g) salmon, bones and skin removed, cut into 1-inch (2.5 cm) pieces
½ lb (250 g) shellfish, such as shell-on shrimp and mussels and shelled scallops
Salt to taste
2 Tbsp (30 mL) finely chopped parsley
1 Tbsp (15 mL) finely chopped oregano
Crostini to serve

This is my take on bouillabaisse. When I made it for the kids when they were little it wasn't always a huge success, but they learned to love it as they got older, and it's now one of our family favorites.
—TERRY GRONER

1. In a large pot over medium heat, sauté the carrots, celery, onion and leek in the oil, until the onion is softened.
2. Stir in the garlic, red chili flakes, bay leaves and saffron.
3. Add the tomatoes, potatoes, white wine and tomato paste. Bring to a boil over high heat, then reduce the heat to medium-low. Simmer until the potatoes are tender, about 20 minutes.

4. Add the stock. Bring to a boil over high heat, then reduce the heat to medium-low. Simmer, uncovered, until the soup thickens, about 30 minutes.

5. While the soup simmers, prepare the rouille (see below).

6. Add the salmon and shellfish to the pot. Simmer, uncovered, over low heat for 10 minutes (or until the mussels have opened, if using). Add salt to taste.

7. Ladle up generous, family-size bowlfuls. Garnish with a scattering of fresh parsley and oregano, and top with crostini spread with rouille.

Rouille

½ cup (125 mL) olive oil
1 sweet red pepper, seeded and diced
1 slice white bread, crust removed
Juice of 1 lemon
1 egg yolk
1 clove garlic
1 tsp (5 mL) Dijon mustard
Salt and pepper to taste

1. Heat a small saucepan over low heat. Add the oil. Gently cook the red pepper until tender, about 30 minutes. Set aside to cool to room temperature.

2. Tear the bread into pieces and place in a food processor, along with the lemon juice, egg yolk, garlic and mustard. Process until smooth.

3. With the motor running, gradually add the olive oil and red pepper. Process until smooth and thick. Add salt and pepper to taste.

Thai Noodle

Lili Scharf
Soup Sister

Makes about 4 servings

4 oz (125 g) thin dried rice vermicelli
  noodles
1 Tbsp (15 mL) vegetable oil
2 Tbsp (30 mL) grated fresh ginger
1 stalk lemongrass, trimmed and cut
  into 2-inch (5 cm) lengths (see sidebar
  on page 119)
Zest of 2 limes
6 cups (1.5 L) chicken stock
2 skinless, boneless chicken breasts,
  thinly sliced (see sidebar)

12 oz (375 g) extra-firm tofu, thickly sliced
3 carrots, peeled and cut into
  matchsticks
2 cups (500 mL) chopped assorted
  fresh mushrooms
1 sweet red pepper, seeded and cut into
  matchsticks
2 Tbsp (30 mL) fish sauce
10 sugar snap peas, trimmed
Juice of 2 limes
Red chili paste to taste

Garnish
1 handful fresh bean sprouts
1 lime, cut into wedges
½ cup (125 mL) crushed roasted peanuts
½ bunch fresh cilantro, roughly chopped

1. Place the vermicelli in a large bowl. Add enough hot water to cover the noodles. Let stand until softened, about 10 minutes. Drain noodles well and set aside.
2. Heat a large pot over medium heat. Add the oil. When the oil is hot, sauté the ginger, lemongrass and lime zest until fragrant, about 30 seconds.
3. Add the stock. Bring to a boil over high heat, then reduce the heat to medium-low. Simmer to blend the flavors, about 10 minutes.
4. Add the chicken, tofu, carrots, mushrooms, red pepper and fish sauce. Bring back to a simmer. Simmer, uncovered, until the chicken is cooked through, about 10 minutes, adding the sugar snap peas at the last minute.
5. Add lime juice, and chili paste to taste. Place some noodles in a large bowl, and cover with a big ladling of fragrant soup with lots of chunky bits. Pile on the garnish of squeaky sprouts, punchy lime, crunchy peanuts and aromatic cilantro.

To slice a chicken breast very thinly, tuck it in the freezer for 15 minutes so it becomes a little frozen. When it's firmed up, it will be easier to slice.

Chunky Chickpea

Klara Meyers
Soup Sister

Makes about 4 servings

3 carrots, peeled and diced
3 stalks celery, diced
1 onion, diced
3 Tbsp (45 mL) olive oil
2 cans (19 oz/540 mL each) chickpeas, drained and rinsed
2 tsp (10 mL) ground cumin
4 cups (1 L) chicken or vegetable stock
Salt and pepper to taste
Tabasco or other hot sauce to taste
½ cup (125 mL) plain yogurt
Paprika for garnish

1. In a large pot over medium heat, sauté the carrots, celery and onion in the oil, until the onion is softened.
2. Stir in the chickpeas and cumin.
3. Add the stock. Bring to a boil over high heat, then reduce the heat to medium-low.
4. Simmer, uncovered, until the carrots are very tender, about 25 minutes.
5. Purée the soup until almost smooth, leaving it slightly chunky. Add salt and pepper and Tabasco to taste.
6. Ladle up a chunky bowl, and garnish with a sloppy swizzle of yogurt and a splashy dash of paprika for color.

My three daughters love this soup on a chilly day. It's easy and uses simple veggies but delivers big taste.
—KLARA MEYERS

Full-Catch Seafood Chowder

Marilou Hamell
Soup Sister

Makes about 6 servings

3 Tbsp (45 mL) olive oil
1 onion, diced
1 leek, white and pale green parts only, washed and sliced
10 thin slices pancetta, diced
2 carrots, peeled and diced
1 fennel bulb, trimmed and diced
1 stalk celery, diced
1 green pepper, seeded and diced
2 cloves garlic, minced or finely chopped
1 small hot red chili, seeded and finely diced
½ cup (125 mL) white wine
Zest and juice of 1 lemon

4 oz (125 g) skinless cod fillet, bones removed
4 oz (125 g) skinless haddock fillet, bones removed
4 oz (125 g) skinless snapper fillet, bones removed
4 oz (125 g) scallops
4 oz (125 g) shell-on shrimp
20 mussels in their shells, scrubbed
¾ cup (185 mL) whipping cream (35% MF)
Salt and pepper to taste
½ bunch parsley, finely chopped

1. Heat a large pot over medium-high heat. Add the oil. When the oil is hot, sauté the onion, leek and pancetta until the onion is browned.
2. Add the carrots, fennel, celery and green pepper. Sauté until the green pepper is softened. Stir in the garlic and chili.
3. Add the wine and cook until the boozy smell disappears.
4. Add 4 cups (1 L) water and the lemon zest and juice. Bring to a boil over high heat, then reduce the heat to medium-low.
5. Gently add the fish, scallops and shrimp to the pot. Finally, add the mussels on top. Simmer, covered, until all the mussels have opened, about 10 minutes. Discard any mussels that don't open completely.
6. Add the cream and reheat gently. Add salt and pepper to taste.
7. Ladle up a brimming bowl of chunky fish chowder, making sure you get to try a little bit of everything. Illuminate the soup with a scattering of fresh green parsley.

This recipe is from my brother-in-law who was a chef. He's retired now and my most favorite thing is to be invited to his house for dinner.
—MARILOU HAMELL

Thai-Spiced Lime and Sweet Potato

Maggie Serpa-Francoeur
Soup Sister

Makes about 6 servings

1 leek, white and pale green parts only, washed and sliced
3 cloves garlic, crushed
1 Tbsp (15 mL) olive oil
6 carrots, peeled and diced
3 sweet potatoes, peeled and diced
1 tsp (5 mL) Thai seasoning (see sidebar)
6 cups (1.5 L) chicken or vegetable stock
1 can (14 oz/398 mL) unsweetened coconut milk
Zest and juice of 1 lime
Salt to taste

1. In a large pot over medium heat, sauté the leek and garlic in the oil, until the leek is softened.
2. Stir in the carrots, sweet potatoes and Thai seasoning.
3. Add the stock. Bring to a boil over high heat, then reduce the heat to medium-low.
4. Simmer, uncovered, until the sweet potatoes are tender, about 30 minutes.
5. Purée the soup until smooth. Add the coconut milk. Reheat over medium heat and add the lime zest and juice, and salt to taste.
6. Ladle up a steamy cup of creamy, sweet soup.

Thai seasoning blends combine ingredients such as chilies, cilantro, ginger, garlic and lime. Look for them in the spice section of your supermarket.

Split Pea with Smoked Dulse

Lynnie Wonfor
Soup Sister

Makes about 6 servings

3 stalks celery, diced
2 carrots, peeled and diced
1 onion, diced
1 tsp (5 mL) dried marjoram leaves
½ tsp (2 mL) dried thyme leaves
3 bay leaves
⅛ tsp (0.5 mL) chipotle chili powder or regular chili powder
2 cups (500 mL) dried split peas
¼ cup (60 mL) Bragg Liquid Aminos (see sidebar)
¼ cup (60 mL) crushed apple-wood-smoked dulse (see sidebar)
⅓ cup (80 mL) apple cider vinegar
¼ cup (60 mL) finely chopped parsley

Bragg Liquid Aminos is a liquid protein concentrate derived from soybeans. Look for it in health food stores. Apple-wood-smoked dulse is a type of seaweed that has been dried over burning apple wood, which imparts a rich, smoky aroma. Try health food stores for this, too.

1. Heat a large pot over medium heat. Sauté the celery, carrots and onion in a splash of water until the onion is softened.
2. Stir in the marjoram, thyme, bay leaves and chipotle powder.
3. Add the split peas, Liquid Aminos and 8 cups (2 L) water. Bring to a boil over high heat, then reduce the heat to medium-low.
4. Simmer, uncovered, until the split peas are tender, about 30 minutes.
5. Add the dulse and simmer for a further 15 minutes. Remove the bay leaves. Add the vinegar.
6. Ladle up a lovely bowlful, and top with a healthy dose of fresh parsley.

Moroccan Red Lentil

Caroline Ishii
Executive Chef and Owner, ZenKitchen, Ottawa

Makes about 8 servings

2 cups (500 mL) red lentils, rinsed
1 onion, diced
2 stalks celery, diced
3 Tbsp (45 mL) olive oil
2 Tbsp (30 mL) grated fresh ginger
5 cloves garlic, minced or finely chopped
1 Tbsp (15 mL) ground cumin
2 tsp (10 mL) sweet smoked Spanish paprika, or more to taste
3½ quarts (3.5 L) vegetable stock
1 can (28 oz/796 mL) tomatoes, roughly chopped
1 bunch dill, roughly chopped
1 bunch mint, leaves roughly chopped
Juice of 1 lemon
Salt and pepper to taste

1. Wash the lentils in several changes of water until the water runs clear. Drain well and set aside.
2. In a large pot over medium heat, sauté the onion and celery in the oil, until the onion is softened.
3. Stir in the ginger, garlic, cumin and paprika.
4. Add the stock and lentils. Bring the pot to a boil over high heat, then reduce the heat to medium-low.
5. Simmer, uncovered, until the lentils are tender, about 35 minutes.
6. Purée half of the soup until smooth. Return to the pot with the chunky lentils.
7. Add the tomatoes with their juices, dill, mint and lemon juice, and heat through gently.
8. Add salt and pepper to taste and more smoked paprika, if liked.
9. Ladle up a hot cup of spicy soup.

Don't add the tomatoes or lemon juice to this soup until after the lentils are tender; the acid in the tomatoes and lemon juice will prevent the lentils from softening.

Mediterranean Medley

vegetarian

gluten free

Dan Hayes
Chef/Owner, The London Chef, Victoria

Makes about 6 servings

½ cup (125 mL) olive oil
2 onions, diced
1 can (19 oz/540 mL) chickpeas, drained and rinsed
4 cloves garlic, minced or finely chopped
1 sprig fresh rosemary, leaves only
1 sprig fresh thyme, leaves only
Pinch of red chili flakes
4 cups (1 L) chicken or vegetable stock
2 cups (500 mL) canned crushed tomatoes
½ cup (125 mL) whipping cream (35% MF)
Salt and pepper to taste

1. Heat a large pot over medium-high heat. Add the oil. When the oil is hot, sauté the onions and chickpeas until the onions are browned.
2. Stir in the garlic, rosemary, thyme and red chili flakes.
3. Remove half of the chickpea mixture to a bowl. Use a fork to crush the chickpeas in the bowl. Set aside to use as a garnish.
4. Add the stock and tomatoes to the pot. Bring to a boil over high heat, then reduce the heat to medium-low. Simmer, uncovered, to blend the flavors, about 30 minutes.
5. Purée the soup until smooth. Add the cream. Reheat over medium heat and add salt and pepper to taste.
6. Ladle up a large and lovely bowl of creamy soup and scatter on some of the cheeky crushed chickpeas.

Fresh herbs team up with canned tomatoes to create a fresh, summery-tasting soup to brighten up the last days of spring.

Glam Clam Chowdère

Pierre A. Lamielle
Cookbook Author

Makes about 4 servings

The recipe blends two very lovely dishes. Underneath is an elegant classic *parmentier* (potato and leek soup), while on top is a flavorful serving of steamed clams.

This glamorous upscale clam chowder is perfect for serving to people when you would like to impress and provide some real substance. It's equally satisfying for dainty ladies who eat martinis for dinner and for salty sea dogs who want to warm their wrinkly waterlogged toes.

—PIERRE A. LAMIELLE

Soup

2 onions, diced
2 leeks, white and pale green parts only, washed and sliced
2 cups (500 mL) peeled and diced russet potatoes
2 cups (500 mL) whipping cream (35% MF)
Salt to taste

Topping

2 Tbsp (30 mL) grapeseed oil
1 dry-cured or fresh chorizo, diced
1 carrot, peeled and diced
1 stalk celery, diced
1 clove garlic, minced or finely chopped
½ cup (125 mL) white wine
2 Tbsp (30 mL) tomato paste
1 lb (500 g) fresh clams in their shells scrubbed
¼ cup (60 mL) parsley leaves

1. For the soup, pile the onions, leeks and potatoes into a large pot. Pour in enough water so the vegetables are completely submerged. Bring to a boil over high heat, then reduce the heat to medium-low.
2. Simmer, uncovered, until the vegetables are very tender, about 35 minutes.
3. Purée the soup until smooth. Add the cream and set aside.
4. For the topping, heat another large pot over medium-high heat. Add the oil. When the oil is hot, sauté the chorizo until browned (and cooked through, if fresh). Stir in the carrot, celery and garlic.
5. Add the white wine and tomato paste. Cook until the boozy smell disappears.
6. Pile in the clams and cover the pot with a lid. Cook until all the clams have opened wide, about 5 minutes. Discard any clams that don't open.
7. Reheat the puréed soup over medium heat and add salt to taste.
8. Ladle up a luscious bowl of creamy soup, top with a glamorous scoop of the clam mixture, and garnish with big parsley leaves.

Easy Green Pea

Marilyn Kraft
Soup Sister

Makes about 6 servings

4 cups (1 L) vegetable stock
1 onion, diced
1½ lb (750 g) frozen peas
Salt and pepper to taste
1 cup (250 mL) sour cream

1. Combine the stock and onion in a large pot. Bring to a boil over high heat, then reduce the heat to medium-low. Simmer, uncovered, until the onion is tender, about 5 minutes.
2. Add the peas and bring back to a boil over high heat.
3. Purée the soup until smooth. Reheat over medium heat and add salt and pepper to taste.
4. Ladle up a steamy bowl of smooth greenery, and garnish with a jaunty dollop of sour cream.

Frozen peas are often more flavorful than fresh peas (except when they're from your own garden, of course). A frozen pea is picked and flash-frozen in the field, shocking its sugars into a frozen state. After picking, fresh peas travel for a day or two to get to the market during which time the peas naturally convert their sugars to starch, which can result in a more bland and boring pea.

The SOUPS of SUMMER

Although we tend to associate soup with colder weather, there's such a cornucopia of dewy fresh produce available in the summer, that it's one of the best times of the year to get soup on. It may sound counterintuitive, but a hot bowl of soup will, in fact, activate your body's natural cooling system. Try not to hang out around the hot stove for longer than you have to, though!

If you can't wrap your head around sipping hot soup in hot weather, there are also some lovely chilled soups here to cool you down. Refreshing and bright, chilled soups are perfect for alfresco entertaining when you want something light to serve as the sun is beating down.

Marvelous Minestrone

Barb Finley
Founder, Project CHEF, Vancouver

Makes about 4 servings

5 new potatoes, scrubbed and diced
1 onion, diced
1 carrot, peeled and diced
1 stalk celery, diced
1 clove garlic, minced or finely chopped
2 Tbsp (30 mL) olive oil
1 tsp (5 mL) finely chopped fresh sage
1 tsp (5 mL) finely chopped fresh rosemary
1 can (19 oz/540 mL) cannellini or romano beans, drained and rinsed
¼ bunch Swiss chard or spinach, stems removed and roughly
   chopped
2 tomatoes, seeded and diced
1 zucchini, diced
4 cups (1 L) chicken or vegetable stock
Salt and pepper to taste
½ bunch parsley, finely chopped

1. In a large pot over medium heat, sauté the potatoes, onion, carrot, celery and garlic in the oil, until the onion is softened.
2. Stir in the sage and rosemary.
3. Pile in the beans, Swiss chard, tomatoes and zucchini.
4. Pour in the stock. Bring to a boil over high heat, then reduce the heat to medium-low.
5. Simmer, uncovered, until the potatoes are tender, about 25 minutes. Add salt and pepper to taste.
6. Ladle up a chunky cup, and garnish with a grandiose scattering of parsley.

vegetarian

Summer Corn Chowder

Robert Stewart
Chef, Four Points by Sheraton Calgary Airport

Makes about 4 servings

1 onion, diced
½ stalk celery, diced
1 clove garlic, minced or finely chopped
1 Tbsp (15 mL) canola oil
2 cups (500 mL) fresh corn kernels
½ sweet red pepper, seeded and diced
½ tsp (2 mL) dried oregano leaves
½ tsp (2 mL) dried thyme leaves
1 bay leaf
3 Tbsp (45 mL) all-purpose flour
1 cup (250 mL) vegetable stock
3 cups (750 mL) milk
1 cup (250 mL) whipping cream (35% MF)
Salt and pepper to taste
2 Tbsp (30 mL) finely chopped parsley

One of the best things about summer is picking fresh corn. Head to a farm and gather a few ears for a fresh, sweet soup that will brighten up an already sunny day.

1. In a large pot over medium heat, sauté the onion, celery and garlic in the oil, until the onion is softened.
2. Stir in the corn, red pepper, oregano, thyme and bay leaf. Sprinkle in the flour and stir to incorporate. Cook, stirring, for 5 minutes.
3. Add the stock. Bring to a boil over high heat. Boil for 1 minute.
4. Add the milk and cream. Bring to a boil, then reduce the heat to medium-low.
5. Simmer, uncovered, until the corn is tender and the soup is smooth and thickened, about 15 minutes. Remove the bay leaf. Add salt and pepper to taste.
6. Ladle up a bubbly cupful, and sprinkle with parsley.

Roasted Corn and Red Pepper Chowder with Chorizo

Avery Trent
Soup Sister

Makes about 6 servings

3 cups (750 mL) fresh corn kernels
1 sweet red pepper, seeded and diced
¼ cup (60 mL) vegetable oil, divided
1 onion, diced
1 dry-cured hot chorizo, diced
2 potatoes, peeled and diced
1 carrot, peeled and diced
1 stalk celery, diced
1 jalapeño chili, seeded and finely diced

2 tsp (10 mL) chili powder
1 tsp (5 mL) ground coriander
1 tsp (5 mL) ground cumin
4 cups (1 L) chicken stock
1 can (14 oz/398 mL) creamed corn
1 cup (250 mL) whipping cream (35% MF)
Juice of 1 lime
Salt and pepper to taste
1 bunch cilantro, roughly chopped

1. Preheat the oven to 350°F (180°C).
2. Line a large rimmed baking sheet with parchment paper. Toss together the corn kernels, red pepper and 2 Tbsp (30 mL) of the oil. Spread the vegetables out in a single layer on the baking sheet. Bake until toasted and slightly charred, about 30 minutes. Remove from the oven and set aside.
3. Heat a large pot over medium-high heat. Add the remaining 2 Tbsp (30 mL) oil. When the oil is hot, sauté the onion and chorizo until the onion is browned.
4. Stir in the potatoes, carrot, celery, jalapeño, chili powder, coriander and cumin.
5. Add the stock and creamed corn. Pile in the roasted corn and red pepper.
6. Bring to a boil over high heat, then reduce the heat to medium-low. Simmer, uncovered, until the vegetables are tender, about 35 minutes.
7. Add the cream and lime juice, and salt and pepper to taste.
8. Ladle up a chunky, handsome bowl, and garnish with a bright sprinkling of cilantro.

For added color, you can add some diced avocado at the last minute.

Summer Greens

Tara O'Brady
Blogger, sevenspoons.net

Makes about 4 servings

1 lb (500 g) zucchini, diced
1 onion, diced
1 shallot, peeled and diced
2 cloves garlic, minced or finely chopped
1 Tbsp (15 mL) olive oil
1 Tbsp (15 mL) unsalted butter

1 lb (500 g) broccoli florets and stems, chopped
4 cups (1 L) chicken or vegetable stock
Green crème fraîche (see below)
2 cups (500 mL) lightly packed baby spinach
Salt and pepper to taste

1. In a large pot over medium heat, sauté the zucchini, onion, shallot and garlic in the oil and butter, until the onion is softened.
2. Pile in the broccoli.
3. Add the stock. Bring to a boil over high heat, then reduce the heat to medium-low.
4. Simmer, uncovered, until the broccoli is tender, about 10 minutes.
5. While the soup simmers, prepare the green crème fraîche (see below).
6. Stir in the spinach until it wilts.
7. Purée the soup until smooth. Reheat over medium heat, and add salt and pepper to taste.
8. Ladle up a bright green bowlful, and garnish with a swirly swizzle of green crème fraîche.

Green Crème Fraîche
1 cup (250 mL) crème fraîche
Zest and juice of ½ lemon
2 Tbsp (30 mL) finely chopped parsley
1 Tbsp (15 mL) prepared horseradish
Salt and pepper to taste

Stir together all the ingredients in a bowl until well combined.

I first made this soup at the end of summer, when zucchini is everywhere and everyone's looking for ways to use it up. It fast became a favorite, with the rich and rounded vegetable sweetness of the soup perfectly complimented by the heat of the horseradish crème fraîche.
—*TARA O'BRADY*

Lemony Lentil and Swiss Chard

Suzanne Husseini
TV Chef and Cookbook Author

Makes about 4 servings

2 onions, diced
¼ cup (60 mL) olive oil
1½ cups (375 mL) Puy lentils (see sidebar), rinsed
5 cups (1.25 L) chicken or vegetable stock
4 potatoes, peeled and diced

3 handfuls thinly sliced Swiss chard leaves (no stems)
1 tsp (5 mL) ground allspice
Juice of 1 to 2 lemons
Salt and pepper to taste
Taklia for garnish (see below)

Puy lentils are small grayish green lentils from France. Look for them in specialty food stores. For a different flavor profile, use 1 Tbsp (15 mL) of crushed Coriander seeds instead of the cilantro in the taklia.

1. In a large pot over medium heat, sauté the onions in the oil, until the onions are softened.
2. Stir in the lentils and mix until glossy.
3. Add the stock. Bring to a boil over high heat, skimming off any scum that rises to the surface.
4. Add the potatoes, Swiss chard and allspice. Reduce the heat to medium-low.
5. Simmer, uncovered, until the potatoes and lentils are tender, about 35 minutes.
6. While the soup simmers, prepare the taklia garnish (see below).
7. Just before serving, add the juice of 1 lemon to the soup, along with salt and pepper to taste. Add additional lemon juice if you think the soup needs it.
8. Ladle up a steamy, simmering dish, and garnish with a fragrant swizzle of taklia.

Taklia

Taklia is a Middle Eastern garnish that's easy to make.

Heat 2 Tbsp (30 mL) **olive oil** in a small skillet over medium heat. Sauté 4 minced or finely chopped cloves **garlic** for about 1 minute until the garlic is fragrant. Add ¼ cup (60 mL) finely chopped **fresh cilantro** and sauté for 1 minute. Spoon the mixture over the soup so it floats nicely on top.

This recipe is excerpted from Modern Flavors of Arabia *by Suzanne Husseini (Appetite by Random House, 2012).*

Lentils, potatoes and Swiss chard are an irresistible trio in this hearty soup. Taklia, which is sautéed garlic and cilantro, is added as the finishing touch to add fragrance and flavor. A squeeze of fresh lemon before serving gives the soup that unmistakable lift and brightness. This soup is ever so comforting.
—Suzanne Husseini

vegetarian

Tortellini with Pesto Cream

Lois Milne
Soup Sister

Makes about 8 servings

2 carrots, peeled and diced
1 onion, diced
½ cup (125 mL) diced red cabbage
2 Tbsp (30 mL) unsalted butter
½ cup (125 mL) white wine
8 cups (2 L) chicken or vegetable stock
2 tomatoes, seeded and diced
1½ lb (750 g) frozen or fresh tortellini
2 cups (500 mL) whipping cream (35% MF)
¼ cup (60 mL) basil pesto
Salt and pepper to taste
¼ cup (60 mL) lightly packed fresh basil leaves, torn into
   small pieces

This easy soup transforms a couple of packages of tortellini into a feast fit for summer company. Just add a salad and great weather to complete the meal.

1. In a large pot over medium-low heat, sauté the carrots, onion and cabbage in the butter, until the onion is softened.
2. Add wine and bring to a boil over high heat. Cook until the boozy smell disappears.
3. Add the stock and tomatoes. Bring to a boil over high heat. Add the tortellini.
4. Reduce the heat to medium-high and cook, uncovered, until the tortellini are tender, about 8 minutes.
5. Add the cream and pesto and bring back to a simmer. Add salt and pepper to taste.
6. Ladle up a steaming green bowl loaded with lots of tortellini and topped with some fresh basil leaves.

Chili-Lime Black Bean

Susan Sampson
Blogger, thefarelady.com

Makes about 4 servings

1 small onion, diced
2 cloves garlic, minced or finely chopped
1 Tbsp (15 mL) olive oil
3 cups (750 mL) vegetable stock
2 cans (19 oz/540 mL each) black beans, drained and rinsed
2 tsp (10 mL) chili powder
2 Tbsp (30 mL) fresh lime juice
Tabasco or other hot sauce to taste
Salt and pepper to taste
¾ cup (185 mL) sour cream
⅓ cup (80 mL) salsa
¼ cup (60 mL) finely chopped cilantro

1. In a large pot over medium heat, sauté the onion and garlic in the oil, until the onion is softened.
2. Add the stock, beans and chili powder. Bring to a boil over high heat, then reduce the heat to medium-low. Simmer, uncovered, to blend the flavors, about 15 minutes.
3. Purée the soup until smooth. Add the lime juice, and Tabasco and salt and pepper to taste.
4. Ladle up steaming bowlfuls and top each with a swirl of sour cream, a spoonful of zesty salsa and a bright sprinkling of cilantro.

This soup makes a great party appetizer ladled into tiny shot glasses or cups, in which case it will serve a lot more people.
—SUSAN SAMPSON

Beet, Apple and Potato

Michael Stadtländer
Chef/Owner, Eigensinn Farm and Haisai, Singhampton, Ontario

Makes about 8 servings

3 Granny Smith apples, peeled, cored and sliced
1 onion, diced
3 Tbsp (45 mL) unsalted butter
6 beets, peeled and diced
2 potatoes, peeled and diced
8 cups (2 L) vegetable stock
2 cups (500 mL) apple juice
Juice of 2 lemons
Salt and pepper to taste
1 cup (250 mL) crème fraîche or sour cream
5 fresh chives, finely chopped

This soup is also fabulous served cold. Just remember, cold soups need a little more salt because they lose flavor when chilled.

1. In a large pot over medium heat, sauté the apples and onion in the butter, until onion is softened.
2. Stir in the beets and potatoes.
3. Add the stock. Bring to a boil over high heat, then reduce the heat to medium-low.
4. Simmer, uncovered, until the beets and potatoes are tender, about 30 minutes.
5. Purée the soup until smooth. Add the apple juice and lemon juice. Reheat over medium heat and add salt and pepper to taste.
6. Ladle up a lovely bowl, and garnish with a dollop of crème fraîche and a cheeky scattering of chives.

Recipe is pictured on page ii.

Bountiful Broccoli

Kimberley Seldon (recipe from Mary Seldon)
Soup Sister

Makes about 4 servings

4 onions, diced
3 Tbsp (45 mL) vegetable oil
4 potatoes, peeled and diced
1 head broccoli, stems diced and head cut into small florets
4 cups (1 L) chicken or vegetable stock
Salt and pepper to taste

1. In a large pot over medium heat, sauté the onions in the oil, until the onions are softened.
2. Stir in the potatoes and broccoli.
3. Add the stock. Bring to a boil over high heat, then reduce the heat to medium-low.
4. Simmer, uncovered, until the potatoes are tender, about 30 minutes.
5. Purée the soup until smooth. Reheat over medium heat and add salt and pepper to taste.
6. Ladle up a bubbly bowlful.

To keep this soup bright green and fresh, make sure you eat all of it on the day you make it. Reheating the soup will dull the color.

Chilled Cherry

Markham Silver
Broth Brother

Makes about 6 servings

⅔ cup (160 mL) granulated sugar
Zest and juice of 1 lemon
2 cinnamon sticks
½ tsp (2 mL) salt
1 lb (500 g) dark sour cherries, stemmed and pitted
½ cup (125 mL) sour cream
1 Tbsp (15 mL) all-purpose flour
Additional sour cream for garnish

Remember that if a dish is to be served cold, you must overseason it as the flavors will diminish when chilled.

1. Combine the sugar, lemon zest and juice, cinnamon sticks and salt in a large pot. Add 6 cups (1.5 L) water. Bring to a boil over medium heat. Boil for 5 minutes.
2. Add the cherries, then reduce the heat to medium-low. Simmer, uncovered, until the cherries are tender, about 15 minutes.
3. Whisk together the sour cream and flour in a medium bowl until smooth. Add a ladleful of cherry soup to the bowl and whisk until smooth. Whisk in another ladleful of soup.
4. Pour the sour cream mixture back into the pot, whisking until well combined.
5. Remove the cinnamon sticks. Purée half of the soup until smooth. Return the puréed soup to the pot.
6. Simmer over low heat, stirring often, until the soup thickens. Add more salt to taste, if necessary.
7. Remove the soup from the heat, pour into a large bowl and let cool to room temperature. Lay a piece of plastic wrap directly on the surface of the soup, covering it completely (this prevents the soup from developing a skin). Chill in the refrigerator overnight. Add more salt and sugar if necessary.
8. Ladle up a cool cup of bright magenta with a dollop of sour cream on top.

The Best Way to Eat Celery

Kevin Kent
Knife Nerd, knifewear.com

Makes about 6 servings

¼ cup (60 mL) unsalted butter
1 head celery, diced
2 onions, diced
5 cloves garlic, minced or finely chopped
Chicken stock or water as needed
½ cup (125 mL) whipping cream (35% MF)
Salt to taste

1. Melt the butter in a large pot over low heat. Add the celery, onions and garlic. Cook, covered, until the celery has softened slightly.
2. Add just enough stock to not quite cover the vegetables. (Too much stock will make this soup watery and boring.) Bring to a boil over high heat, then reduce the heat to medium-low.
3. Simmer, uncovered, until the celery is tender, about 35 minutes.
4. Purée the soup until smooth. Add the cream. Reheat over medium low heat and add salt to taste.
5. Ladle up a handsome bowl of punchy celery flavor.

When adding stock or water to this soup, think of a very rocky stream. Remember, rocks in a stream do not float. The stock should not reach the top of the veg. You don't want floating veg or you'll have weak soup. What we want here is a huge punch of celery.
—KEVIN KENT

Gazpacho de Tomate

Gilles Brassart and Dominique Moussu
Co-owners, Cassis Bistro, Calgary

Makes about 6 servings

   7 tomatoes, seeded and diced
   3 sweet red peppers, seeded and diced
   3 stalks celery, diced
   2 English cucumbers, peeled, seeded and diced
   3 shallots, peeled and diced
   1 cup (250 mL) sherry vinegar
   Salt to taste
   ⅓ cup (80 mL) olive oil
   Tabasco or other hot sauce to taste
   Pepper to taste

1. Combine the tomatoes, red peppers, celery, cucumbers and shallots in a large nonreactive bowl.
2. Add the vinegar and salt to taste. Toss to coat well.
3. Cover the bowl with plastic wrap and marinate in the refrigerator for at least 2 hours.
4. Purée the vegetable mixture until smooth. With the motor running, add the olive oil in a slow, steady stream.
5. Pour the soup into a large nonreactive bowl and add Tabasco, pepper and more salt to taste.
6. Pour forth a lovely frosty glass of chilled soup.

This chilled Spanish soup is the perfect way to cool down on a steamy summer's day.

Split Mung Bean with Tomato and Cilantro

Meeru Dhalwala
Co-owner, Vij's and Rangoli, Vancouver

Makes about 6 servings

1 cup (250 mL) dried split mung beans or yellow lentils, rinsed well
1 Tbsp (15 mL) grated fresh ginger
1 tsp (5 mL) turmeric
1 bunch spinach, roughly chopped
1 onion, diced
1 Tbsp (15 mL) cumin seeds
⅓ cup (80 mL) vegetable oil
2 tomatoes, diced
½ tsp (2 mL) red chili flakes
1 bunch cilantro, finely chopped
Salt to taste

If you're put off by the word *mung*, you'll be missing out on a very good opportunity to try a delicious bean that's slightly off the beaten bean path. Mung beans create a really luscious, almost gelatin-like richness when cooked.

1. Combine the mung beans, ginger and turmeric in a large pot. Add 6 cups (1.5 L) water. Bring to a boil over high heat, skimming off any foam that rises to the surface.
2. Reduce the heat to medium-low. Simmer, covered, until the mung beans are tender, about 2 hours.
3. Stir in the spinach and remove the pot from the heat. Cover and set aside.
4. In a large skillet over medium heat, sauté the onion and cumin seeds in the oil, until the onion is softened.
5. Stir in the tomatoes and red chili flakes. Sauté until the tomatoes are softened.
6. Add the onion mixture to the soup, along with the cilantro. Add salt to taste.
7. Ladle up a gorgeous bowlful.

Curried Tomato and Potato

vegetarian

gluten free

Sandi McCrory
Soup Sister

Makes about 6 servings

2 lb (1 kg) tomatoes, diced
6 whole cloves garlic
1 Tbsp (15 mL) curry powder
¼ cup (60 mL) olive oil, divided
2 lb (1 kg) potatoes, peeled and diced
2 tsp (10 mL) dried thyme leaves
4 cups (1 L) chicken or vegetable stock, divided
½ cup (125 mL) whipping cream (35% MF)
Juice of 1 lemon
Salt and pepper to taste

1. Preheat the oven to 400°F (200°C). Line 2 large rimmed baking sheets with parchment paper.
2. Toss the tomatoes and garlic with the curry powder and 2 Tbsp (30 mL) of the oil. Spread out in a single layer on one baking sheet.
3. Toss the potatoes with the thyme and the remaining 2 Tbsp (30 mL) oil. Spread out in a single layer on the second baking sheet.
4. Put both baking sheets in the oven. Roast until slightly browned and the potatoes are tender, about 45 minutes.
5. Purée the tomatoes with half of the stock until smooth. Transfer the purée to a large pot.
6. Purée the potatoes with the remaining stock until smooth. Add to the pot.
7. Add the cream. Reheat over medium heat and add the lemon juice and salt and pepper to taste.
8. Ladle up a bowlful of pleasing pink potage.

Roasting the tomatoes will concentrate all their sweetness and make this soup deeply yummy. Roasting the potatoes will add a toasted baked-potato flavor that's so distinct. Together they join forces to make a rich and complex soup experience.

Broccoli, Spinach and Leek

Sharon Pertman
Soup Sister

Makes about 6 servings

4 leeks, white and pale green parts only, washed and sliced
¼ cup (60 mL) unsalted butter
2 heads broccoli, stems diced and heads cut into small florets
2 potatoes, peeled and diced
8 cups (2 L) chicken or vegetable stock
1 pkg (10 oz/300 g) frozen spinach
Salt and pepper to taste
Freshly grated Parmesan cheese for garnish (optional)

1. In a large pot over medium heat, sauté the leeks in the butter, until the leeks are softened.
2. Stir in the broccoli and potatoes. Sauté for 5 minutes.
3. Add the stock and frozen spinach. Bring to a boil over high heat, then reduce the heat to medium-low.
4. Simmer, uncovered, until the potatoes are tender, about 25 minutes.
5. Purée the soup until smooth. Reheat over medium heat and add salt and pepper to taste.
6. Ladle up a simmering green bowlful, and top with cheese if you like.

This is my go-to recipe whenever I need something to do to take my mind off things, or whenever I think someone else might also need to!
—*SHARON PERTMAN*

European-Style Pea, Carrot and Dill

Val Bracey
Soup Sister

Makes about 8 servings

3 quarts (3 L) chicken or vegetable stock
2 cups (500 mL) split peas
3 potatoes, peeled and diced
2 carrots, peeled and diced
2 stalks celery, diced
1 onion, diced
½ cup (125 mL) finely chopped parsley
3 Tbsp (45 mL) finely chopped fresh dill
2 tsp (10 mL) celery seeds
Salt and pepper to taste

1. Combine the stock, split peas, potatoes, carrots, celery and onion in a large pot. Bring to a boil over high heat, then reduce the heat to medium-low.
2. Simmer, uncovered, until the peas are tender and falling apart, about 1 hour.
3. Stir in the parsley, dill and celery seeds.
4. Purée the soup until smooth. Reheat over medium heat and add salt and pepper to taste.
5. Ladle up a steamy potage of thick and hearty soup.

Since we are doing things in the European style, you'd better get yourself a big loaf of rustic hand-kneaded bread. Tear off a piece, spread it with the best unsalted butter you can find, sprinkle on some crunchy salt (Maldon salt would be perfect) and enjoy with the soup.

Sweet Potato and Corn

Debra Adelman
Soup Sister

Makes about 6 servings

1 onion, diced
1 sweet red pepper, seeded and diced
2 Tbsp (30 mL) olive oil
2 cloves garlic, minced or finely chopped
1 small hot red chili, seeded and finely diced
2 tsp (10 mL) ground cumin
2 cups (500 mL) fresh corn kernels
1 sweet potato, peeled and diced
8 cups (2 L) vegetable stock
Salt and pepper to taste
1 lime, cut into wedges

1. In a large pot over medium heat, sauté the onion and red pepper in the oil, until the onion is softened.
2. Stir in the garlic, chili and cumin. Stir in the corn and sweet potato.
3. Add the stock. Bring to a boil over high heat, then reduce the heat to medium-low.
4. Simmer, uncovered, until the sweet potatoes and corn are tender, about 25 minutes.
5. Purée half of the soup until smooth. Return the puréed soup to the pot. Reheat over medium heat and add salt and pepper to taste.
6. Ladle up a steamy, chunky bowl of sweet soup, and squeeze over a fresh and zesty lime wedge.

The fresh, full flavors of the sweet potatoes and corn will satisfy both vegetarians and meat eaters.

Canadian Summer Gazpacho

Sandy Martin
Soup Sister

Makes about 4 servings

6 tomatoes, peeled and cut into chunks
1 large English cucumber, peeled and cut into chunks
1 onion, cut into chunks
1 green pepper, seeded and cut into chunks
4 whole cloves garlic
2¼ cups (560 mL) tomato juice, divided
¼ cup (60 mL) olive oil
Zest and juice of 1 lemon
½ tsp (2 mL) chili powder
½ tsp (2 mL) dried basil leaves
Salt to taste

This chilled soup keeps well in the refrigerator for several days if you store it in a tightly closed jar. Add additional finely chopped vegetables just before serving, if desired.

1. In a food processor and using on-off pulses, process the tomatoes until finely minced. Transfer to a large nonreactive bowl.
2. Repeat the process with the cucumber, onion and green pepper, adding each in turn to the bowl.
3. With the food processor's motor running, drop the garlic through the feed tube and process until minced.
4. Add half of the tomato juice, the oil, lemon zest and juice, chili powder and basil to the garlic in the food processor. Process until smooth.
5. Add the tomato-juice mixture to the bowl, along with the remaining tomato juice. Add salt to taste.
6. Cover and refrigerate for several hours for the flavors to blend.
7. Ladle up a frosty bowlful to enjoy on a hot summer's day.

Spiced Carrot and Coconut

Lynn Whitestone
Soup Sister

Makes about 4 servings

1 onion, diced
2 cloves garlic, minced or finely chopped
1 tsp (5 mL) ground coriander
1 tsp (5 mL) ground cumin
2 Tbsp (30 mL) vegetable oil
3 carrots, peeled and diced
3 parsnips, peeled and diced
4 cups (1 L) vegetable stock
1 Tbsp (15 mL) tamarind paste (see sidebar)
1 can (14 oz/398 mL) unsweetened coconut milk
Salt and pepper to taste

1. In a large pot over medium heat, sauté the onion, garlic, coriander and cumin in the oil, until the onion is softened.
2. Pile in the carrots and parsnips.
3. Add the stock. Bring to a boil over high heat, then reduce the heat to medium-low.
4. Simmer, uncovered, until the parsnips and carrots are tender, about 30 minutes. Stir in the tamarind paste.
5. Purée the soup until smooth. Add the coconut milk. Reheat over medium heat and add salt and pepper to taste.
6. Ladle up a dreamy, creamy sweet cupful.

Tamarind paste is made from the sweet-sour pulp of the tamarind fruit. It's a popular flavoring in South Asian cuisines where it's used much the same way as lemon juice is in the west. Look for it in Indian, Pakistani or Thai grocery stores.

Roasted Heirloom Tomato

Disnie Zivot
Soup Sister

Makes about 4 servings

2 lb (1 kg) assorted heirloom tomatoes, halved
1 onion, quartered
3 whole cloves garlic
2 Tbsp (30 mL) olive oil
10 fresh basil leaves
3 fresh sage leaves
1 sprig fresh oregano, leaves only
Pinch of red chili flakes
2 cups (500 mL) chicken or vegetable stock (approx.)
1 Tbsp (15 mL) balsamic vinegar
Salt and pepper to taste
⅓ cup (80 mL) freshly grated Parmesan cheese

1. Preheat the oven to 375°F (190°C). Line a large rimmed baking sheet with parchment paper.
2. Toss the tomatoes, onion and garlic with the olive oil, and spread out in a single layer on the baking sheet. Roast until slightly browned, about 45 minutes.
3. Add the basil, sage, oregano and red chili flakes to the tomatoes.
4. Purée the tomato mixture until smooth. Transfer to a large pot and add enough stock to give a soupy consistency.
5. Bring the soup to a simmer over medium heat. Add the balsamic vinegar, and salt and pepper to taste.
6. Ladle up a bubbly red bowl of nostalgic tomato soup, and garnish with a gentle dusting of grated Parmesan cheese.

Heirloom tomatoes come in many shapes, sizes and flavors. Making this soup is a great excuse to buy a whole assortment. Their textures vary widely and it can be a lot of fun trying all the different kinds. As you're chopping the tomatoes, do a little taste test of your own! You can top this soup with a sprig of the herb of your choice—basil or thyme are our favorites.

Summer Minestrone with Basil Swirl

Bonnie Stern
Cookbook Author and Columnist

Makes about 6 servings

1 leek, white and pale green parts only, washed and thinly sliced
2 cloves garlic, minced or finely chopped
Pinch of red chili flakes (optional)
1 Tbsp (15 mL) olive oil
2 zucchini, diced
2 stalks celery, diced
8 cups (2 L) vegetable stock
1 small head broccoli, stem removed and head cut into bite-size florets

½ lb (250 g) fresh green beans, sliced
½ cup (125 mL) small soup pasta
2 cups (500 mL) packed chopped kale or Swiss chard leaves, or whole spinach or arugula leaves (optional)
1 cup (250 mL) fresh or frozen peas
3 green onions, sliced
Salt and pepper to taste
½ cup (125 mL) coarsely grated Parmesan cheese
Basil swirl (see below)

Because of minestrone's robust flavor and deep tomato-red color, most people think the soup belongs in the fall. But minestrone can change with the seasons, and here's a greener, lighter summer version. If you overcook it, the vegetables may discolor but it will still taste great. And the basil swirl delivers a great flavor punch.

—BONNIE STERN

1. In a large pot over medium heat, sauté the leek, garlic and red chili flakes (if using) in the oil, until the leek is softened.
2. Stir in the zucchini and celery. Sauté for 1 minute.
3. Add the stock, broccoli and beans. Bring to a boil over high heat. Add the pasta and kale or Swiss chard (if using). Cook, uncovered, until the pasta is tender, about 5 minutes.
4. Add the peas, spinach or arugula (if using) and green onions. Cook, uncovered, until the peas are tender and the spinach wilts, 2 to 3 minutes. Add salt and pepper to taste.
5. Ladle up a veggie-packed portion, sprinkle with cheese and stir in about 1 Tbsp (15 mL) of basil swirl.

Basil Swirl

Combine 1 cup (250 mL) packed **fresh basil leaves** and 1 clove **garlic** in a food processor and process until finely minced. With the motor running, gradually add ⅓ cup (80 mL) **olive oil** through the feed tube and process until smooth. Add **salt** to taste.

Leek, Corn and Pepper Chowder

Janet Uffelman
Soup Sister

Makes about 6 servings

3 leeks, white and pale green parts only, washed and sliced
1 sweet red pepper, seeded and diced
2 Tbsp (30 mL) unsalted butter
2 cups (500 mL) fresh corn kernels
Pinch of cayenne
6 cups (1.5 L) chicken or vegetable stock
½ cup (125 mL) whipping cream (35% MF)
Salt and white pepper to taste
3 Tbsp (45 mL) finely chopped parsley
Tabasco or other hot sauce to taste

1. In a large pot over medium heat, sauté the leeks and red pepper in the butter, until the leeks are softened.
2. Pile in the corn and stir in the cayenne.
3. Add the stock. Bring to a boil over high heat, then reduce the heat to medium-low.
4. Simmer, uncovered, until the vegetables are tender, about 25 minutes.
5. Add the cream. Reheat over medium heat and add salt and pepper to taste.
6. Ladle up a chunky bowl of creamy chowder. Garnish with some cheeky parsley, and pass around the Tabasco.

Get your corn as fresh as possible. Pick your own if you have to. It takes only 20 minutes for a picked ear of corn to start converting its sugars to starch, so to ensure the corn is at its sweetest, it must be picked at its peak and cooked quickly.

Beety Eight-Vegetable Borscht

Eric Akis
Cookbook Author, everyonecancook.com

Makes about 8 servings

2 lb (1 kg) beets, trimmed
1 onion, diced
1 carrot, peeled and diced
1 large stalk celery, diced
2 cloves garlic, minced or finely
  chopped
2 Tbsp (30 mL) vegetable oil
4 cups (1 L) vegetable stock
3 cups (750 mL) vegetable juice,
  such as V8 or Mott's Garden
  Cocktail

2 potatoes, peeled and diced
1 cup (250 mL) fresh corn
  kernels
1 bay leaf
4 oz (125 g) fresh green beans,
  cut into 2-inch (5 cm) pieces
2 Tbsp (30 mL) finely chopped
  fresh dill
Salt and pepper to taste
Sour cream or thick plain yogurt
  for garnish

A veritable cornucopia of summer veggies stars in this hearty meatless borscht. Change them up depending on what looks good at your local farmers' market.

1. Place the beets in a large pot with enough cold water to cover them by 2 inches (5 cm). Bring to a boil over high heat, then reduce the heat to medium-low. Simmer, covered, until the beets are tender, about 40 minutes.
2. Cool the beets under cold, running water. Remove the peel, then cut the beets into ½-inch (1 cm) cubes and set aside.
3. In a large pot over medium heat, sauté the onion, carrot, celery and garlic in the oil, until the onion is softened.
4. Add the beets, stock, vegetable juice, potatoes, corn and bay leaf. Bring to a boil over high heat, then reduce the heat to medium-low. Simmer, uncovered, until the potatoes are just tender, about 15 minutes.
5. Add the beans. Simmer, uncovered, until the beans are just tender, about 5 minutes. Remove the bay leaf. Add the dill, and salt and pepper to taste.
6. Top beautiful bowls of the borscht with a dollop of sour cream or yogurt.

Soup Sisters

Warming hearts...one bowl at a time

About Soup Sisters

Soup Sisters is a nonprofit, charitable social enterprise dedicated to providing comfort to women and children through the making, sharing and donating of soup to designated women's shelters.

The concept is simple. Groups or individuals register to participate in a soup-making event at a local professional kitchen under the guidance of a chef facilitator. At each event, participants produce 150 to 200 servings of nourishing soup that are delivered fresh to a local women's shelter. A representative from the recipient shelter is also there to talk about issues surrounding family violence and domestic abuse.

Gathering with others in the community to help women and children in crisis is what's gratifying about participating in these events. Corporate groups, book clubs, professional colleagues, neighborhood associations and just simply friends celebrating a milestone are a sampling of the kinds of groups that have registered for soup-making events. Events are social evenings with lively conversation, chopping, laughter and warm kitchen camaraderie that culminate in a simple, sit-down supper of soup, salad, bread and a glass of wine. (Yes, there is soup for everyone!)

The tremendous response to the work Soup Sisters are doing across the country is powerful evidence that communities throughout Canada are taking a strong and united stand against domestic abuse and family violence. Women's-shelter freezers from east to west are chock-full of Soup Sisters' homemade soup.

Broth Brothers was launched in the fall of 2009 as an extension of the Soup Sisters soup-making family and in support of homeless youth who are transitioning from street life into mainstream society.

Through selected youth shelters and counseling centers, Broth Brothers provide young people with nourishing and nurturing soup and let them know that their community cares for them and believes in their potential.

Soup Sisters and Broth Brothers are year-round programs that allow people across the country to transform their community contributions into a meaningful experience and a tangible way to give. Both are 100-percent volunteer-driven and self-sustaining, which means our work substantially decreases the operating costs of the shelters we support.

Please contact us at info@soupsisters.org to inquire about launching Soup Sisters or Broth Brothers in your hometown. To find out more about where we are currently operating, visit our website at www.soupsisters.org.

All royalties from *The Soup Sisters Cookbook* will go to support our operations as we help to meet the needs of women, children and youth across the country, with a homemade bowl of soup.

Soup Sisters in Action

From the humble beginnings of a soup-making birthday celebration for Sharon Hapton's 50th birthday, Soup Sisters now supports more than twenty women's emergency shelters and programs for youth-in-crisis in ten cities across Canada. Here's how we make a difference:

"When you're afraid and alone, confused and overwhelmed, sometimes what you need most is something simple, a small kindness, an uncomplicated gift, a wordless sign that somebody, somewhere, has you in their thoughts. Each time a Youth Emergency Shelter Society (YESS) client sits down to a hot bowl of homemade soup, they receive a message of encouragement, compassion and reassurance that renews their hope and determination when they desperately need support."
—*Emily Keating, YESS, Edmonton*

"Interval House of Ottawa offers a safe haven for women and their children fleeing abuse. Our staff try to make their stay as comfortable and as homey as possible during this difficult time. Once a month, we receive bowls of nourishing soup from Soup Sisters for our residents and their children. What is more comforting than a bowl of soup? It's nourishing to the body, the heart and the soul.

Through these bowls of soup, women are told that they are cared for by others; that there are kind and generous people out there who are willing to give up time from their busy schedules to make soup for them; that they matter! At a time when our women and children are feeling alone, distraught, mistrustful, confused and unloved, a bowl of soup means the world to them. It helps to reaffirm their trust in humanity and in people's ability to be kind."
—*Laura McCrae, Interval House of Ottawa*

"We are so grateful that Soup Sisters chose to support Marillac Place. The soups are delicious, nutritious and very much appreciated by the mothers who reside here. Each bowl sends a heartwarming message to our mothers that the community cares about and supports them."
—*Angela Murdock, Marillac Place, Kitchener, ON*

"Soup Sisters provides soup to the Salvation Army Kate Booth House, a program for women and their dependent children who are at risk of experiencing or have experienced violence. The soups bring comfort and nourishment to physical bodies and, just as importantly, to the souls of those who have been hurt.

This gift reminds women and children that the world can be kind, and there are people who care. In this way, Soup Sisters contributes to making our community a stronger, healthier place."
—*Captain Jennifer Hillier, The Vancouver Homestead and Kate Booth House, The Salvation Army, British Columbia Division, Vancouver*

"Every month we get a special delivery of soup made by our incredible friends at Soup Sisters. The soup is not just a meal for the women and children at Interval House, it's also a symbol of warmth and caring. We are so honored to receive soup and support from the community, and the impact it has on our families is huge.

Most people don't know that Interval House doesn't have a cook.

Every day, women take turns making dinner for 30 people. Being able to defrost and serve the soup cooked by Soup Sisters can lift the weight off a woman's shoulders and turn a busy night into a relaxing one.

Sharing meals together is an important step in the healing process. It helps break the isolation that is so common among women who've been abused. By delivering healthy soups, our friends at Soup Sisters are also sharing a meal with our residents, and the impact of their actions is felt with every spoonful!"
—*Ashleigh Saith, Interval House, Toronto*

"Oshki Kizis Lodge (OKL) is the only First Nation, Inuit and Métis shelter in the National Capital Region. The donation provided by Soup Sisters is not simply soup, it's a generous demonstration that there are many people in the community who want to support women fleeing violence, and support them in a very personal way. The soups are enjoyed by all the shelter residents and we have also been able to provide soup to women moving to their own homes. Some of the soup has even been distributed to women accessing the outreach van, which operates out of the shelter, serving women who are homeless or at risk of homelessness.

On behalf of all the women and children residing at the shelter, as well as the staff and board of Minwaashin Lodge, we say, "*chi meegwetch*"—a huge thank-you—to the founders of Soup Sisters and to the many volunteers who come together each month to selflessly share their time to create so much more than pots of soup."
—*Frances Daly, Oshki Kizis Lodge, Ottawa*

"Once a month, Soup Sisters help to feed the women and children staying at the Calgary Women's Emergency Shelter. The considerable amount of healthy soup that is provided to us helps defer our operating expenses. Just as important, the knowledge that this soup is made specifically for them by fellow Calgarians is vital as they begin their new lives free of abuse.

Not so obviously, Soup Sisters is helping to reduce family violence in our community by raising awareness of abuse and our organization. Bringing individuals together to cook, have fun and socialize helps to strengthen healthy relationships, which are the foundation of a strong community. Through Soup Sisters' events, our organization now has the unique opportunity to create a dialogue with thousands of new people about family violence and about the resources we can offer to those who may be experiencing abuse or know someone who is.

Soup Sisters will be held up for many years as an example of how to create a stronger community. We thank Sharon and her volunteers for the considerable impact she is having on ending family violence in Calgary."
—Lisa Falkowsky, *Calgary Women's Emergency Shelter*

"My name is Coleen. I just moved into the Kelowna Women's Shelter two days ago. I work full-time and it's been a real challenge trying to make it to work and deal with the chaos in my life, and with the huge depression that lingers relentlessly night and day and keeps me from sleeping. I just wanted to say how nice it was to be able to take a bowl of comforting minestrone soup to work—one less thing to worry about. I tend not to eat much these days, but it was all made and ready to microwave. So please accept my humble thanks for your love, generosity and kindness when I truly need and appreciate it most."
—*Coleen (last name withheld), Kelowna, B.C.*

Acknowledgments

It's been a crazy three years building a cross-country soup-making organization that now supports more than 20 women's and youth shelters and which, to date, has supplied over a hundred thousand bowls of soup to women, children and youth in crisis. None of this could have happened without the love and support of some very special people who helped Soup Sisters come into being.

I come from a family of four kids—three girls and a boy, the baby of the family. When we were young my mother always said, "And just remember, I never opened a can!" We would all just look at her and say, "Okay, Mom." None of us understood then what she meant. Now I realize my mother was telling us that she was taking care of us in the most meaningful way she knew, by providing us as best she could (times were lean) with wholesome food made with love.

So, my first thanks goes to my mom, Terry Groner, who is, and always has been, an amazing cook. She survived some really harsh times as a child in World War II France and came to Canada as a young immigrant bride. As I look back, I realize that Soup Sisters is a testament to her core belief that, through food, we take care of each other in the most nurturing of ways. The soup speaks for itself.

My deepest thanks go out to my actual sisters, Lili Scharf and Rina Grunwald, who are always with me every step of the way, making me laugh and cry in equal measures, and who are ridiculously proud of me. Then, there is my friend Laura Martin, who is like my third sister. It's no exaggeration to say that she has spent hundreds of selfless hours listening, encouraging, advising and mentoring while I plunged into the making of this beautiful thing called Soup Sisters.

Special thanks to my wonderful daughter, Blaire, who was the first person with whom I ever shared the words "Soup Sisters." She was 18 at the time and told me that the name was "very, very corny." She now joins me at as many launches as possible and volunteers often. I have to smile now, almost four years since that first conversation, when I catch her bragging about her mom on Facebook. And thanks, too, to my son, Dan, who quietly understands my every thought, challenges my ideas and shares my soul.

Since our mandate is to support survivors of domestic abuse, I am sometimes asked if I come from an abusive marriage. I have had the most privileged marriage imaginable to a husband, friend and colleague of 30 years. My husband, Garry, supports me to the highest degree and in the most simple and loving ways. Whenever I have really long workdays, he helps with the grocery shopping and laundry, and keeps me grounded while I obsess for hours over soup.

I have met truly incredible people throughout Canada, who came to me as total strangers because they saw something in Soup Sisters that resonated with them. To the tireless local coordinators who show leadership every day by organizing monthly events across the country: I feel as though I have known you all my life and I am so privileged and humbled to call you my dear friends.

My thanks to Pierre A. Lamielle for his support, creativity and illustrations; to Julie Van Rosendaal for her stunning interpretations of how a Soup Sisters soup looks; and to Caren McSherry for giving *The Soup Sisters Cookbook* concept to Robert McCullough and for her huge ongoing support of our organization. Thanks go also to Robert McCullough and Lindsay Paterson of Appetite by Random House for enthusiastically supporting me over the months that it took to compile and edit all the amazing soup recipes; to Julia Aitken for interpreting and editing the recipes with great care and detail; and to all the Soup Sisters, chefs and food professionals from across the country who submitted their favorite soups.

Many thanks also to Susan Burns of Random House of Canada, to Leah Springate and Scott Richardson for designing the cover and interior, to Shallon Cunningham for the cover photograph and to copyeditor Grace Yaginuma.

For the photographs of the Soup Sisters events included in this book, I'd like to thank the following: Annemarie Gruden (Ottawa),

Mark Rabo (Toronto), Mercedes Verriere (Victoria), Romy Young (Edmonton), Monique de St. Croix (Calgary) and Mandy Anderson (Vancouver).

Finally, I offer my heartfelt thanks to the many hundreds of women and men from all walks of life who stand shoulder to shoulder sharing chopping, stirring and seasoning duties with great cheer, heart and enthusiasm . . . all to produce "love" in a bowl.

A "souper" huge thanks to everyone!

Index